THE
Kinesthetic
CLASSROOM

This book is dedicated to my mother, who will always be the wind beneath my wings, to M. B. P. for being my greatest gift, to my devoted family and the Anthonys for their unconditional love and support, and to my faithful friends for their strength and encouragement.

Traci Lengel

I would like to dedicate this book to my wife and children, my greatest teachers, who bring me profound joy each day; to my mom, dad, and sisters for their love and enduring support; and to Don and Diana for being my educational role models and inspirations.

Mike Kuczala

THE
Kinesthetic
CLASSROOM

Teaching and
Learning Through
Movement

TRACI LENGEL // MIKE KUCZALA
FOREWORD BY JEAN BLAYDES MADIGAN

A JOINT PUBLICATION

CORWIN
A SAGE Company

RTC
Regional Training Center
A higher degree of learning

For information:

Corwin
A SAGE Company
2455 Teller Road
Thousand Oaks, California 91320
(800) 233-9936
Fax: (800) 417-2466
www.corwinpress.com

SAGE Ltd.
1 Oliver's Yard
55 City Road
London EC1Y 1SP
United Kingdom

SAGE Pvt. Ltd.
B 1/I 1 Mohan Cooperative
 Industrial Area
Mathura Road, New Delhi 110 044
India

SAGE Asia-Pacific Pte. Ltd.
33 Pekin Street #02-01
Far East Square
Singapore 048763

Printed in the United States of America

Library of Congress Cataloging-in-Publication Data

Lengel, Traci.
The kinesthetic classroom: teaching and learning through movement/Traci Lengel, Mike Kuczala; foreword by Jean Blaydes Madigan.
    p. cm.
"A Joint Publication with the Regional Training Center."
Includes bibliographical references and index.
ISBN 978-1-4129-7954-2 (pbk.)

   1. Movement education. 2. Movement, Psychology of. 3. Brain stimulation. 4. Academic achievement. I. Kuczala, Mike. II. Regional Training Center. III. Title.

GV452.L46 2010
372.868—dc22   2009047377

This book is printed on acid-free paper.

10 11 12 13 14 10 9 8 7 6 5 4 3 2 1

Acquisitions Editor:	Hudson Perigo
Associate Editor:	Julie McNall
Editorial Assistants:	Brett Ory and Allison Scott
Production Editor:	Veronica Stapleton
Copy Editor:	Codi Bowman
Typesetter:	C&M Digitals (P) Ltd.
Proofreader:	Dennis W. Webb
Indexer:	Sheila Bodell
Cover Designer:	Scott Van Atta

Contents

Foreword

It's in the news daily! America is in an obesity epidemic, and it presents a great danger to our youth. Children spend a great deal of time sitting. They belong to the new sedentary society of *sitness*, not fitness! But neuroscience is telling a different story. Exercise boosts brain function (Medina, 2008). Students who are more physically fit perform better academically (Texas Education Agency, 2009). Exercise grows brain cells (Ratey, 2008). Movement facilitates cognition (Sylwester, 1995). This seems contradictory. If exercise helps the brain to learn, then why aren't we adding movement, physical activity, and exercise to the school day to put brains and bodies back into balance? How can the neuroscience that supports the link of movement to learning translate into classroom practice? Can we give every child every advantage to learn? How can we create healthy, active learners who are ready and eager to learn and do it without sacrificing time and standards?

We can find the answers to these questions in this book by Traci Lengel and Mike Kuczala, who collaborated to bring educators a very useful tool for teaching. Traci and Mike combine their expertise to provide interesting insight into how the brain learns, and then they translate that information into classroom practice. The concepts presented are brain based and brain compatible and apply to learners of all ages. The research presented is understandable and applicable to all students. The activities are purposeful, easy to interpret, and fun for the teachers and the students. Each chapter concludes with an outline of key points discussed in the chapter, a wonderful reference tool for busy educators.

Compelling research supports the link of movement to improved cognition. Dr. John Ratey's (2008) research findings show how exercise improves learning and why teachers should use movement in the classroom to enhance learning and memory. But some teachers are still skeptical or uneasy about how movement can help their students or improve test scores. They ask several questions, including the following:

Will movement take too much time away from my lessons?

Will I lose control of student behavior?

What if I am not a good "mover" myself?

How can this meet the standards I am supposed to teach?

The authors address these concerns and many more to alleviate any misgivings about movement strategies. Their concepts show how movement in the classroom *adds to* the learning process rather than *distracts from* it and can prepare the brain for better retention and retrieval.

The central theme of the book is *controlled movement with purpose*. The authors outline many purposes for movement including the following:

- Preparing the brain with specific movements may improve communication from one part of the brain to another
- Providing brain breaks can give the brain the opportunity it needs to process and consolidate information
- Supporting exercise and fitness encourages healthy living
- Developing class cohesion through movement activities can prepare the brain for learning new information
- Reviewing content through movement during the lesson may be an ideal way to use repetition to improve retention
- Teaching new content through movement will help many students of all ages and cultures to understand and retain information

Some of the most helpful ideas presented are in the classroom management section. This is an area where all teachers benefit, especially when accommodating movement in a classroom setting. Another favorite section of mine provides activities, each one demonstrating movement with purpose. There is a variety of activities using many subject areas for all grade levels. In my experience of teaching academics kinesthetically, I have seen students who previously struggled in the traditional classroom "click on" when they were allowed to express themselves through activities like these. It is indeed a joy to behold!

I have been in education for more than 30 years, both in the classroom and as a physical educator. My belief is that every child *can* learn. I also believe that every child's level of health and wellness *can* be improved. My experience has shown that when we use movement to anchor learning, the child's understanding of the concept becomes stronger by far.

I truly appreciate the inclusion of the success story of our Action Based Learning Lab in Traci and Mike's book. The action-based learning lab shows how controlled movement with purpose can help fill in developmental gaps to prepare the brain for learning. The data we have collected are amazing and show the power that movement, physical activity, and exercise can have on the developing brain. I also see how teaching academic concepts kinesthetically in the classroom and using exercise and physical activity to teach academics in the gymnasium builds a bridge of cohesiveness for the student.

And for me, that's the purpose of teaching: the increased health and the learning of each student.

Educational research tells us that a majority of school-age students are predominately kinesthetic processors. They crave movement to understand concepts. That's why this book is an important addition to any personal or professional teacher library. It is a comprehensive reference to how students learn and how to accommodate their learning through movement. I know you will find *The Kinesthetic Classroom: Teaching and Learning Through Movement* useful and informative and a valuable resource to help your students work at their best!

In JOY!
Jean Blaydes Madigan
NeuroKIDnesiologist
Action Based Learning

Preface

From your genes to your emotions, your body and brain are dying to embrace the physical life. You are built to move. When you do, you'll be on fire.

—Dr. John Ratey (2008)

*T*he Kinesthetic Classroom: Teaching and Learning Through Movement is a resource that provides all teachers, in every content area and grade level, with a quick means to finding information and ideas on how to implement movement in the classroom to enhance the teaching and learning process. It supports the notion of educating the child as a whole. The suggested activities all provide opportunity for students to grow cognitively, socially, mentally, emotionally, and physically. Six distinct purposes for using movement in the classroom will be shared. The sequential steps in this framework known as *movement with purpose* are listed next:

1. Preparing the brain

2. Providing brain breaks

3. Supporting exercise and fitness

4. Developing class cohesion

5. Reviewing content

6. Teaching content

These are supported by cutting-edge educational research explaining the benefits of using movement as a method in the teaching and learning process. Never before has education been so focused on standards, curriculum, and content. This book will serve as a critical tool for delivering those very components in a teacher, student, and brain-friendly manner. We hope that you allow this framework to become the standard for using kinesthetic activities and movement to support and enhance curriculum objectives. These activities should be included in all classrooms committed to engaging the learner and differentiating through learning style, interest, and/or readiness.

Chapter 1 discusses both the modern student and transforming the learning environment. The six purposes of movement and the research supporting each provide a direct route to combating the current educational and health concerns of children. An extensive graphic organizer explains this six-step framework allowing teachers to progress in the implementation of movement at their own pace. Teachers' comfort levels regarding movement in the classroom may vary greatly. In this chapter, guidance is provided at a pace that is individualized.

Chapter 2 focuses on important, easy-to-understand information describing the brain-body connection. The relationship between how the brain learns and the role movement plays in this process is closely examined. Success stories are shared to highlight that combining physical activity, movement, and academics leads to educational growth and success. Ten critical reasons for implementing the six purposes of movement are carefully described.

One serious concern regarding movement is classroom management. Chapter 3 is dedicated to this concern. It addresses the unmotivated and hypermotivated student, safety concerns, and transfer time from movement to seat. Tips and strategies will be shared to better manage student behavior during movement activities.

Chapters 4 through 9 are action packed with 170 movement activities that can be implemented in the classroom. Each chapter focuses on one of the six purposes of movement. Suggestions are easy to follow and practical. Movement activities are appropriate for various grade, fitness, and ability levels. Recommendations are made on how to adapt and customize certain activities. Usually, little or no equipment is needed. A particular emphasis is placed on the capability of transferring movement activities from one subject to another.

Chapters 4 through 6 focus on initiating movement in the classroom. Ninety-four movement activities that can be performed in two minutes or less are described. This is a perfect place for the cautious teacher to begin. Planning is minimal, and little time is taken away from academic content. These activities are great for reenergizing the body and brain. After participating in these activities, the brain refocuses and learning becomes more efficient.

Chapter 7 addresses the importance of building a classroom environment through class cohesion. Although these 14 activities are not intended for daily use, they serve a critical role. Students who feel safe and comfortable in a learning environment are more capable of optimal learning. Therefore, allowing students the opportunity to engage in these activities is advantageous to the learning process.

Chapters 8 and 9 concentrate on curriculum. The 62 activities contained in these chapters are designed to expose teachers to a different way of thinking. To teach and review content through movement, teachers must be willing to stray from traditional teaching techniques. Many of these movement activities are intended to supplement teaching methods already being used. Sometimes, a suggested activity may actually replace a current teaching practice. Either way, students are learning and reviewing academic content through exciting and stimulating means.

Chapter 10 serves as a cornerstone for creating an environment that truly educates the whole child. By adopting this philosophy, students' cognitive, social, and physical well-beings are enhanced. Learning through movement and/or participating in physical activities will occur on a daily basis. The message that good health and active living are essential and fundamental will be clearly received. We hope that learning will become more efficient, student test scores will improve, and behavior challenges will decrease. Most important, a new joy of learning will emerge.

Acknowledgments

We would like to give special thanks to the following people:

- Jean Blaydes Madigan for writing the foreword and sharing insights on Chapter 4
- Acquisitions editor Hudson Perigo for her advice, guidance, and belief in this project
- John Parkin, Diana Ramsey, and The Regional Training Center for copublishing this book and guiding the dynamic organization that made all this possible
- Maribelle Bitler for her generous wisdom
- Heather Anthony, Sue Rose, Jessica Parry, and Shannon Robinson for their support, guidance, and inspiration
- Dale Miller, Lee Oberparleiter, and Jim Gilbert for their support, expertise, and friendship
- Jerry Moyer for the "fight," the friendship, and the faith
- Susan Nelson for her tutelage, friendship, guidance, and the opportunity to learn how to write
- Kathleen Anthony and Todd Anthony for their direction, encouragement, and collaboration
- All the wonderful, creative students who have helped us shape and develop our teaching methodologies
- All the teacher participants who have been through our graduate courses. You have no idea how much we have learned from you! We thank you for putting knowledge to work in classrooms

Special Recognition: Because of the nature of our profession and experiences with movement, it was very difficult to know the original creators of many of the activities contained herein. We would like to thank anyone who originated an activity and was not recognized for it. Please know that this was very difficult for us, but we greatly appreciate the movement activities as well as their brilliant creators.

PUBLISHER'S ACKNOWLEDGMENTS

Corwin Press gratefully acknowledges the contributions of the following reviewers:

Ingrid L. Johnson, Assistant Professor
Grand Valley State University
Allendale, MI

Sarah Kinsella, Physical Education Teacher
Cape Elizabeth Middle School
Portland, ME

Rob McMahon, NSCA CSCS, Physical Education Teacher and Strength
    Coach
Montgomery Blair High School
Silver Spring, MD

Kristy Spears, Fourth-Grade Teacher
Fort Mill School District
Fort Mill, SC

Deborah Stevens-Smith, Associate Professor
Clemson University
Clemson, SC

Diane Whaley, Associate Professor, Curry School of Education
Director, Lifetime Physical Activity Program
University of Virginia
Charlottesville, VA

About the Authors

 **Traci Lengel** is a health and physical education teacher in the Pocono Mountain School District. With more than 16 years of experience, Traci's knowledge in motor development, lifelong fitness, health education, and curriculum development has contributed to the success of her insightful educational programs. Additionally, Traci is an adjunct professor of graduate education at Gratz College of Pennsylvania and The College of New Jersey. In conjunction with this position, she is coauthor/designer of two graduate courses with Mike Kuczala. These highly esteemed graduate courses, titled *Wellness: Creating Health and Balance in the Classroom* and *The Kinesthetic Classroom: Teaching and Learning Through Movement*, have had a profound effect on the personal and professional lives of thousands of educators. Known for her innovation, enthusiasm, and work ethic, Traci devotes much of her time to her personal and professional successes. With her motivational teaching methodology, she presents and facilitates workshops for professional development programs in the areas of wellness, stress management, enhancing student thinking, and teaching and learning through movement. Her ultimate professional challenge is to inspire educators at all levels to incorporate movement into their daily teaching.

Traci's greatest joy is the unconditional love and support she shares with her family and friends.

 **Mike Kuczala** is the assistant director of instruction for the Regional Training Center, an educational consulting firm based in Randolph, New Jersey. He is the designer of *Motivation: The Art and Science of Inspiring Classroom Success*, a graduate course offered to teachers in Pennsylvania, New Jersey, and Maryland. Also an American Fitness Professionals and Associates Certified Nutrition and Wellness Consultant, he has coauthored two other graduate courses with Traci Lengel: *Wellness: Creating Health and Balance in the Classroom* and *The*

Kinesthetic Classroom: Teaching and Learning Through Movement. As an adjunct professor of graduate education at Gratz College of Pennsylvania and The College of New Jersey and an in-demand keynote presenter, he regularly facilitates professional development programs in the areas of motivation, using movement to enhance the learning process, brain-based instruction, differentiated instruction, enhancing student thinking, multiple intelligences, and topics related to wellness and stress management. His entertaining and practical professional development programs have been enjoyed by thousands of teachers and administrators over the last decade.

He is married to Cyndy, a former elementary classroom teacher. They are the parents of twin children Scott and Demi. He can be reached at mkuczala@thertc.net.

1

Introduction to Movement With Purpose

⇨ Is movement becoming a necessity in today's classroom?

⇨ How often do students need to move and are attention spans rapidly shrinking?

⇨ What are the six purposes of movement?

⇨ Can I incorporate the purposes of movement in my classroom and are there practical, hands-on examples showing me how?

⇨ What is the framework for movement with purpose?

⇨ Where do I go from here?

IS MOVEMENT BECOMING A NECESSITY IN TODAY'S CLASSROOM?

As the responsibilities of the educator continue to grow, one might ask, how do I fit it all in? The demands are time consuming as teachers make an effort to accomplish the following:

- Differentiate instruction
- Teach to the standards

- Incorporate data-driven instruction
- Improve standardized test scores
- Vary assessments
- Create modifications to meet student needs

Although the weight of these challenges is great, the most difficult task may be educating the child as a whole with the intention of generating productive, successful members of society. This assumes the educator's role goes beyond teaching academic content. They must also teach life skills such as these:

- Communication
- Anger management
- Decision making
- Conflict resolution
- Behavior management
- Health and well-being

These skills have become part of today's curriculum. Is society changing? How is the rapid growth in technology affecting the way children's brains think and learn? These questions are important to consider as we watch students grow and develop. Technology is presenting information to the brain in an exciting and stimulating manner. Is education keeping up with this current trend?

Movement in the classroom provides both teacher and student with a stimulating classroom environment. Allowing students to get out of their seats to move while learning provides the novelty and change the brain seeks. It also provides the opportunity for students to grow cognitively, physically, mentally, emotionally, and socially. There are many incentives to use movement to accomplish the various challenges faced on a day-to-day basis. By using movement, academic standards can be met, test scores can be improved, and important life skills can be developed.

To obtain the benefits of movement in a classroom setting, an understanding of the six different purposes for getting students out of their seats must be gained. A developed appreciation of how to use movement to accomplish distinct goals offers the opportunity to actively engage students in the learning process. Students will no longer sit and listen for the entire period; they will move to learn academic concepts, people skills, and higher-level thinking strategies. Six specific purposes for movement in the classroom will be clearly explained in this chapter. By building an awareness of the many opportunities that movement provides, it is feasible to believe that movement is becoming a necessity in today's classroom.

HOW OFTEN DO STUDENTS NEED TO MOVE?

For many children, spending too much time watching television, playing video games, or surfing the Internet will have a detrimental effect on their attention span (Healy, 1990). Determining a child's attention span is difficult because it can vary from child to child and subject to subject. Therefore, no conclusive study has consistently measured a child's ability to stay focused on a particular task. Typically, children's attention spans are related to their age. On average, it has been reported to be three to five minutes per year (Schmitt, 1999). For example, kindergarten students' attention spans may range from approximately 15 to 20 minutes. Many theorists have also concluded that the average attention span of an adult is 15 to 20 minutes. These findings have been debated because the individual's level of interest must be taken into consideration. It appears as though the research is showing us the attention span of an adult can be comparable to that of a child—or are we suggesting that students have a longer attention span than they actually do? Because researchers have not yet incorporated all the factors affecting attention span, their findings are more useful, at this point in time, for creating general guidelines than for determining the attention span of any one individual.

Trying to determine how often students need to move in a particular class period or throughout the day is not an easy task. Children who are raised in stimulating, active environments produce more neural connections in the brain (Bruer, 1991). When the body is inactive for 20 minutes or longer, there is a decline in neural communication (Kinoshita, 1997). The following considerations must be weighed:

- How many of my students are diagnosed with attention deficit disorder (ADD), attention deficit hyperactivity disorder (ADHD), or other learning disabilities?
- What appears to be the average attention span of the students in my classroom when they are interested in the topic and/or activity?
- What appears to be the average attention span of the students in my classroom when they are not interested in the topic and/or activity?
- How much material can I cover in a particular time where my students can comprehend, process, and retain the information?
- How many learners in my classroom prefer kinesthetic learning?

Though no one particular existing formula can be used to determine how often students need to move, evidence is making it clear that movement allows students to refocus and strengthen their ability to pay attention. Researchers at the University of Illinois found that school-age students were better able to allocate attentional resources following vigorous walking (Mitchell, 2009). These same researchers also found a "meaningful difference" in reading, spelling, and math achievement tests following exercise. The important question to consider is, who is responsible for student learning states? If a child is not paying attention in class, who is at fault, the teacher or the student—perhaps both? Students must take some responsibility to develop self-discipline while using strategies to stay focused and on task. On the other hand, teachers are in charge of creating and facilitating an environment that engages, motivates, and challenges the learner. If a student's mind begins to wander during class time, then it is possible the lesson and/or the way it is being taught is simply not holding the child's interest.

Because it can be difficult to determine how often and how long students should move in a given time, it is critical to search for signs that students are losing focus. The following list provides some examples of signs students display when they are having difficulty staying focused:

- Staring off into space
- Fidgeting, wiggling hands and feet
- Humming
- Doodling
- Talking to a neighbor
- Shouting answers before the question is completed
- Acting out by breaking class rules
- Displaying attention-getting behaviors
- Failing to follow directions accurately or completely
- Inability to finish activities
- Interrupting others

Identifying these signs will assist in determining when students need to move their body so they can refocus and reenergize their brain. Ideally, a teacher who uses the six purposes of movement effectively and consistently can prevent students from becoming distracted and losing their attention. Students who use their body while gaining knowledge are actively engaged in the learning process. If attention span is rapidly shrinking, it is reasonable to believe the six purposes of movement may be the perfect resource for combating this concern.

WHAT ARE THE SIX PURPOSES OF MOVEMENT?

Purpose 1: Prepare the Brain

Can certain physical movements actually stimulate and prepare the brain for learning? This concept examines what is called whole-brain learning and is derived from research on how the brain learns. As part of this conceptual framework, many researchers and theorists believe that specific, directed physical movements help prepare the brain for leaning or improve brain function. Although some view this research as young and inconclusive, others feel it is a solid combination of brain science and common sense. One of the goals of a brain-compatible classroom is to establish a brain-friendly learning environment. Some of these characteristics are listed next:

- Establishing safe and supportive surroundings
- Offering a rich, stimulating atmosphere
- Providing a community approach
- Creating opportunities for group learning
- Making sure students are hydrated
- Allowing the brain to make connections while purposefully using transfer
- Incorporating rehearsal and practice
- Working within memory time and capacity limits
- Incorporating movements that facilitate cognition

As brain researchers continue the important work of understanding how children learn, there are signals that brain development is enhanced through movement. Preparing the brain for learning incorporates specific brain-compatible movements that improve neural connections. In other words, neurons (brain cells) can communicate more effectively so cognitive abilities are heightened. Although the research is promising, the philosophy presented in this book supports the notion that these specific movements may stimulate the brain as intended but also serve as effective brain breaks and activities that support exercise and fitness. Therefore, a win-win approach is established.

It is believed the way we think, learn, and remember can be directly influenced by the physical movements in which we participate (Ratey, 2008). There are specific programs that provide evidence that these activities are beneficial and effective in preparing the brain and enhancing the learning process. Two specific examples, *action based learning* and *learning readiness PE,* will be discussed in the following chapter. Exercises that cross the midline of the body along with movements that stimulate the vestibular system and improve spatial awareness will be emphasized. The classroom activities found in Chapter 4 can be used to develop this purpose of movement.

Each hemisphere of the brain controls the opposite side of the body. A thick bundle of 250 million nerve fibers called the corpus callosum connects the two hemispheres and allows them to communicate. Crossing the midline, also known as cross laterals, refers to moving the arms and/or legs across the body from one side to the other. These integrative movements help students prepare for learning by forcing the hemispheres to work together, assisting in energy and blood flow, decreasing muscle tension, and stimulating and focusing the brain to improve concentration

(Dennison & Dennison, 1988; Hannaford, 1995; Promislow, 1999). The eyes also move in various pathways similar to the limbs (Dennison & Dennison, 1988). This is called visual tracking. Tracking is the ability of the eyes to follow an object. If brain hemispheres are not efficiently communicating with each other, reading can be difficult. Although there is limited technical research on these movements, the logic supporting them is very powerful (Jensen, 2000).

Many children who experience learning disabilities struggle with crossing the midline of their body. These students will often have difficulty with reading and writing (Pica, 2006). By incorporating cross-lateral movements into your classroom regimen, you may help improve these skills. Although there is no guarantee, these activities can't hurt and will probably energize your students (Jensen, 2000). Although humans do not strictly prefer the left or right hemisphere, most people have a dominant side. Cross-lateral activities can help students use both sides of their brain while improving skills they are lacking. Learning how to read and write, thinking clearly, and problem solving are skills that involve both hemispheres of the brain.

The vestibular system provides the brain with meaningful information. This visual system is related to motion or the position of the head and body in space. The vestibular system accomplishes two major tasks. First, it contributes to an individual's sense of equilibrium and conveys information to the muscles and posture. Second, it controls eye movements so images remain steady and in focus. This explanation helps to rationalize a connection between the vestibular system and academic skills. The vestibular system is most critical for cognition and is the first sensory system to develop (Jensen, 2000). As a result, it serves as an organization tool for other brain processes while playing a key role in perception. Therefore, balance problems can hinder brain function.

Spatial awareness allows us to sense both objects in the space around us and our body's position in space. Without this awareness, students may have difficulty with the following:

- Reading
- Organizing written work
- Understanding abstract math concepts
- Reproducing patterns and shapes

Studies have suggested a connection between abstract thinking and a well-developed sense of spatial awareness. The developing brain needs to activate this system adequately so movement and cognitive growth can develop (Jensen, 2000). Various spinning, balancing, jumping, rolling, turning, and combination activities can help develop and improve the vestibular system and spatial awareness. Movements that stimulate the inner ear alert the brain to sensory stimuli (Hannaford, 1995). The more senses that are used for learning, the more likely information will be stored and retrieved from memory.

Purpose 2: Provide Brain Breaks

The goal of a brain break is exactly what it sounds like: to give the brain a break from academic content. This can be a frightening proposition because of the pressure to cover a large amount of material in a given time; there is just no time to give the brain a break. Or is there? Often, the demand to get through material is so great that teachers catch themselves starting to simply "cover" material. Are students learning the material that is required of them? Maybe it is time to examine and prioritize students' needs for learning.

The important role that repetition plays in learning a concept goes without question, but what else does the brain need? Consider how the brain actually learns from a physiological standpoint. Approximately 90% of the oxygen in our body/brain is stale unless we take a deep breath, yawn, or get up and move. A lack of oxygen can result in confusion and concentration and memory problems (Blaydes Madigan, 1999). This needs to be contemplated as we facilitate learning. Here are some reasons to include brain breaks during lessons:

- To give the hippocampus, in part responsible for short-term memory and navigation, time to process information
- To lessen feelings of being overwhelmed by content
- To provide the opportunity for laughter and fun
- To refocus the brain as students return to the content
- To develop social skills
- To reenergize the body and the brain

Purpose 3: Support Exercise and Fitness

Does it seem reasonable to ask a teacher that does not have a background in physical education to bring fitness into their classroom? If your initial response is no, consider the following questions:

- Are we raising the first generation of children who may not outlive their parents? Many experts have claimed this to be possible. As an educator, does that thought concern you?
- Would increased activity in the classroom help control the significant rise in the obesity epidemic?
- How much time do students receive physical activity or physical education class in your school?
- Has recess been decreased or taken away from children?
- If students sit from the time they enter class until they leave, what message is being sent?

- Is there something I can do in my classroom to encourage fitness along with a healthy, active lifestyle?
- What kind of role model am I in regard to supporting the health and well-being of my students?

The idea of adding exercise and fitness to your classroom is a new phenomenon that is getting attention. The importance of this concept varies from state to state and school to school. Although some schools are limiting the amount of activity students receive, others are creating laws that students must receive 30 minutes of continuous physical activity every school day (Winterfeld, 2007). Ideally, this movement would come from a physical education teacher and/or class. Unfortunately, space and time make this nearly impossible. Hence, classroom teachers are encouraged to open their minds to the idea of exercise in the classroom.

This purpose of movement need not be made into a tribulation, as it does not suggest that teachers engage students in a full body, head-to-toe workout. Simply getting students up on their feet and doing several quick exercises may be all it takes. In 60 seconds or less, you can have your students participate in a physical activity, such as jogging in place, which can refocus their brain while giving it a burst of fresh oxygen. Think of the critical message a student receives about fitness if exercises are performed in every class they attend. Researchers suggest that physically fit children perform better in the classroom. Research also shows a correlation between academic skills and physical fitness scores. Therefore, if students perform well on physical fitness assessments, they may also score well academically (Ratey, 2008). Recent studies in both California and Texas suggest that physically fit students do better on standardized tests. It is irresponsible to ignore this research any longer. Incentives for exercise and fitness in the classroom include the following:

- Providing a brain break
- Energizing the body and refocus the brain
- Improving students' health and well-being
- Improving academic achievement through enhanced brain function
- Improving fitness levels
- Improving mental/emotional well-being
- Learning more efficiently
- Reducing stress

Purpose 4: Develop Class Cohesion

How important is the emotional climate in a classroom related to students' ability to learn new information? It is imperative to consider how the brain prioritizes information. The information most crucial to the brain is related to survival. If a student's survival needs are not met, the brain is not in a position to work at optimal levels. The second most important information to the brain is that which generates emotions. What is the emotional state of students in your classroom, and can you manage this state? If students are feeling stressed or uncomfortable, it is very difficult for the brain to learn new information. The parts of the brain that use higher-level thinking strategies and critical-thinking skills shut down when an individual's emotional state is compromised. The third priority of the brain is receiving data for new learning. Therefore, the emotional climate in your classroom plays a major role in a student's ability to learn new information (Sousa, 2006).

What key ingredients help produce an environment that may enhance the classroom's mental and emotional state? Humor and/or music can have a great effect on the emotional state of students. However, movement is the number one manager of student learning states (Jensen, 2000). Is it possible that movement will have that much effect on one's learning state? Think back to the last time you sat for a long period to learn something new. What was your emotional state?

How students get along with one another while in your classroom plays a direct role in their learning state. If your classroom is viewed as a fun, safe environment where students are kind and supportive of one another, learners have a greater chance of finding academic success. Consider a classroom that is strictly business. In this environment, there is no time to build social skills and develop class cohesion. Will students learn and grow at optimal levels in this situation? Which learning environment would you personally desire?

Taking time to engage students in movement activities that will develop class cohesion is important. Some benefits for engaging students in class cohesion activities are listed below:

- Providing the brain with a much needed break
- Improving communication and listening skills
- Providing an opportunity for problem solving and higher-level thinking
- Offering an environment that promotes laughter and fun while engaging learners
- Improving motivation and discipline
- Heightening students' interest in attending and participating in class
- Building relationships and a general concern for one another
- Developing a sense of belonging
- Improving self-esteem

Purpose 5: Review Content

Many teachers spend a respectable amount of time reviewing previously taught concepts. Why not review material through movement? Movement is exciting and can make learning fun, engaging, and emotional.

When cognitive information is linked with movement, retaining, and recalling, the data become easier (Hannaford, 1995). Memories and neural pathways fade when they are not used (Jensen, 1998). Providing multiple opportunities to review content is essential to the learning process. Therefore, reviewing concepts can take place at the beginning, middle, and end of each lesson. Combining the review of material with movement can easily be implemented throughout lessons.

The beginning of any given lesson is often spent reviewing previously taught material. If students are moving during content review, they will awaken their bodies as well as their brains. How much time should be spent reviewing material at the beginning of class? The first 10 minutes is ideal for teaching new concepts (Sousa, 2006) when the brain is typically focused and ready to learn something fresh. Therefore, spending a long time reviewing previously taught concepts at the beginning of the lesson may not be the best use of time. However, a quick movement activity that allows students to review information and focus the brain can be very effective. An activity of this type can motivate and prepare the brain to dive into something new.

Reviewing material during the middle of class by using movement is ideal. Benefits of reviewing content through movement include the following:

- Providing an opportunity to use repetition to improve retention
- Allowing time for the brain to process and consolidate new information
- Presenting time for the brain to rejuvenate
- Improving motivation and discipline
- Waking up the body and brain as they begin to feel tired and sleepy
- Creating a fun and exciting learning environment
- Allowing students the chance to engage in a social environment

Previously taught material is often covered toward the end of a lesson. The last five minutes of class time is actually a great opportunity for teaching another new concept or reminding the brain of the most important concept that was taught during the current lesson. Does movement make sense here? It depends on how long your students have been sitting. If movement was used throughout the lesson, it may not be necessary. However, if students have been sitting for a long time, it may be the perfect opportunity to review content using movement.

Purpose 6: Teach Content

Can I teach this academic concept through movement? This is an important purpose of movement to consider. Allowing students to use movement to grasp a new concept may be extremely beneficial and aid in retention of material. *Learning by doing* can be a very powerful example of implicit learning. Eric Jensen (2000) describes a few reasons for increasing the amount of implicit learning in a classroom setting:

- More information can be absorbed and may last longer.
- Every age group can learn and obtain implicit knowledge.
- There is a cross-cultural transmission.
- Bridges may be formed that connect the body and brain.

Recall the first time you learned something new. Compare times when you heard information explicitly, perhaps through a lecture, versus a time when you learned something implicitly, like riding a bike. Think about the process of learning. Did using your body to ride the bike actually help you to learn the concept? If someone just lectured to you about how to ride the bike, would you be able to ride it? Implicit learning activates the body and brain simultaneously so both learning and the retention of information take place with greater ease.

Movement should be considered whenever teaching a new concept or standard. Using movement and physical activity in the learning process will help many students recall information more efficiently (Blaydes Madigan, 1999). This does not mean getting students on their feet to move into cooperative learning groups for an activity, going to the board to write something, or moving students' seats. Think deeper; this refers to actually experiencing the academic concepts by using the body. Here are a few simple examples:

- Understanding a comma: Students walk while saying a sentence and pause to represent the purpose of a comma
- Understanding number sequence: Students stand up and represent a number sequence by using their bodies
- Understanding a war: Students role-play the war
- Understanding an atom: Students become the atom

This challenge may vary from subject to subject. Keep in mind, movement does not need to replace your usual way of teaching a given concept. If you traditionally lecture, have students discuss the topic, read, or complete a worksheet; these methods can still be used effectively. However, these methods can be altered or shortened so there is time to allow students to learn the concept through movement. Here are some benefits for teaching new content through moment:

- Increase understanding and retention
- Improve social skills and class cohesion
- Increase learner motivation
- Provide opportunities for problem solving and higher-level thinking
- Stimulate the brain/body connection

CAN I INCORPORATE THE PURPOSES OF MOVEMENT IN MY CLASSROOM AND ARE THERE PRACTICAL, HANDS-ON EXAMPLES SHOWING ME HOW?

Yes! You can do this!

You may be saying to yourself right now, "This sounds great, but can I do this?" Some apprehension might stem from the following questions:

- Do I have the personality to make this work?
- Can I still have effective classroom management?
- Will movement make learning more efficient?
- Will I have enough space?
- Will I be able to maintain a safe environment?

The answer to all of these questions is yes! Although these concerns are genuine and understandable, they can be overcome through time, patience, and solid proof that movement is one of the most effective ways to teach, and reach, students of all ages and abilities.

Please refer to the graphic organizer (Figure 1.1). There are three important areas to consider on this chart: (1) the educator's individual comfort level, (2) how to use movement, and (3) a suggested order in which the purposes of movement might be implemented. Progress through the levels of this chart should occur at an individual rate that feels comfortable. Personality type and experience with movement could result in a personal alteration in the chart. For example, if you do not exercise on a regular basis, you may feel more comfortable developing class cohesion before you are ready to support exercise and fitness. Educators who consider themselves advocates of movement may be more inspired to move through the levels at a quicker pace. However, you must choose the pace that is right for you!

If the concept of movement in a classroom is difficult for you to grasp, you need to start slowly, trying simple activities that will help you increase your comfort level. Any given activity may have more than one purpose. For instance, the purpose of students participating in 10 chair-dips is to support exercise and fitness. However, this quick activity also provides a brain break. This graphic organizer serves as a guideline for the order in which the purposes of movement might be explored. Purposes were placed in this order based on the following considerations:

- Teacher preparation
- Amount of class time activity/purpose might take
- Level of creativity
- Potential classroom management challenges
- Challenge level for implementation

WHAT IS THE FRAMEWORK FOR MOVEMENT WITH PURPOSE?

Figure 1.1 Movement With Purpose

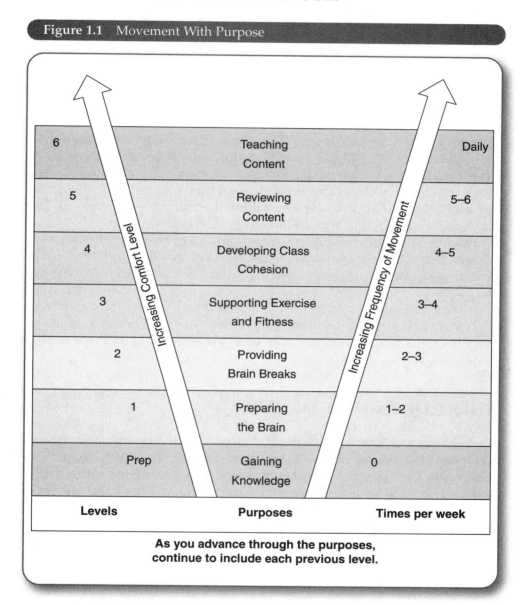

Levels	Purposes	Times per week
6	Teaching Content	Daily
5	Reviewing Content	5–6
4	Developing Class Cohesion	4–5
3	Supporting Exercise and Fitness	3–4
2	Providing Brain Breaks	2–3
1	Preparing the Brain	1–2
Prep	Gaining Knowledge	0

Increasing Comfort Level *Increasing Frequency of Movement*

As you advance through the purposes, continue to include each previous level.

The first level is known as the prep stage. This is where knowledge development and an understanding of the six purposes of movement are critical. The more you learn, the more eager you will be to try movement activities in your classroom.

Level 1 (preparing the brain), Level 2 (providing brain breaks), and Level 3 (supporting exercise and fitness) are the easiest places to start. These three purposes of movement are the least risky and require little or no creativity on behalf of the teacher. They demand little planning time and can be performed quickly. If you are nervous or hesitant to move students, try engaging them in an activity that prepares the brain for learning or a brain break once a week for a month. Take note of how your students respond to the activities. Remember to pay attention to student learning states before and after the movement. Look for signs that show your students are benefiting from the activities. Watch for any improvements in test scores or motivation in your classroom.

Once you recognize the benefits of movement, you will become more comfortable and encouraged to increase the frequency of movement in your classroom. Level 4 (developing class cohesion) and Level 5 (reviewing content) may take a little more planning and classroom management. As you explore these two purposes, you will rejoice as your student's test scores increase while you continue to reach state and national standards. You will notice that you are not falling behind in your content and students are eager to learn in an interconnected environment.

The most difficult and perhaps most important purpose of movement is Level 6 (teaching content). This purpose requires time, effective classroom management, planning, and creativity. You may want to try this later, once your confidence has strengthened. Take small steps and start slow. Remember the very reason you became a teacher and the importance of providing a positive learning experience. Teachers want to reach as many students as they can, and movement is a teaching tool that simply cannot be ignored.

WHERE DO I GO FROM HERE?

The remaining chapters of this book will focus on the brain/body connection, classroom management, safety, and various examples on how to incorporate the six purposes of movement in an academic setting. This book can be used as a resource for ideas or a simple tool that provides knowledge and support. It is important, however, that you begin to consider and critique your lessons. This process will allow you to create and design lessons in which movement can best serve you and your students.

Thinking outside the box is encouraged when it comes to the concept of movement in a classroom. Some will have a natural ability to do this. On the other hand, this will be a true challenge for others. Be patient and understand that this style of teaching will not develop overnight. Time and trial and error are two key components that are essential for future success. It is likely that you will involve students in movement activities that do not go the way you planned. Don't give up! Allow yourself to learn from mistakes. As improvement happens, you will be able to implement the six purposes of movement into your classroom with ease. The work that you may have to do to get to that point may be easier said than done; however, the rewards will be endless, and your students will thank you for years to come!

Chapter 1 Recap

- Educators can accomplish their goals in the classroom while incorporating the six purposes of movement. Movement is becoming a necessity in today's classroom.

- Teachers need to look for signs that students are losing focus. Movement can regain that focus and possibly prevent students from losing it in the first place.

- Purpose 1: Preparing the brain for learning incorporates specific brain-compatible movements that can improve neural connections.

- Purpose 2: Providing brain breaks can give the brain the opportunity it needs to process and consolidate information.

- Purpose 3: Supporting exercise and fitness encourages healthy living. Based on current research, physically fit children perform better academically, and therefore, providing exercise in the classroom can help to improve school performance.

- Purpose 4: Developing class cohesion through movement activities can prepare the brain for learning new information.

- Purpose 5: Reviewing content through movement during the lesson is an ideal way to use repetition to improve retention.

- Purpose 6: Teaching content through movement will help many students of all ages and cultures understand and retain information.

- Look ahead for information on the brain-body connection, classroom management, safety, and multiple examples on how to incorporate the six purposes of movement into a classroom setting. Prepare to be patient, creative, and ready to think outside the box.

2

The Brain-Body Connection

⇨ In education, should the brain and body be addressed separately or together?

⇨ How does the brain learn, and how can movement help this process be more efficient?

⇨ Can physical activity, movement, and academics be combined to enhance the learning process?

⇨ How does action research support movement in the classroom?

⇨ What are 10 critical reasons why educators should use the six purposes of movement to improve learning?

IN EDUCATION, SHOULD THE BRAIN AND BODY BE ADDRESSED SEPARATELY OR TOGETHER?

One hundred years from now, historians may look on current life as an age where the exciting possibilities of the brain-body relationship were finally realized. Each year brings new evidence supporting the notion that the two have been mistakenly assumed as separate entities. The fact is that they flow to and through each other, as an extension and a reflection of the other's will. Time will tell how this understanding might affect medicine and education: how doctors diagnose and how teachers design learning. Here are some ideas to consider:

- Biomedical research is shedding light on the delicate balance between the immune system and the stress response, which in large part has a psychological premise. The brain and the immune system continuously signal each other (Sternberg & Gold, 2002). State of mind may prove extremely important in both illness recovery and resistance.
- In his book *SPARK: The Revolutionary New Science of Exercise and the Brain,* John Ratey (2008), Harvard associate clinical professor of psychiatry, describes exercise as "Miracle-Gro" for the brain. One significant study showed that aerobic exercise was as effective as antidepressants in treating depression.
- In the classroom, schools across the United States are showing remarkable academic progress because of the introduction of serious fitness programs.
- It is common for the amateur and professional athletes to improve their athletic performance through mental imagery that highlights the idea that the body will fall in line with carefully planned visual images of physical success.

These examples represent the power of the brain-body connection and emphasize the importance of understanding and utilizing the connection between the two. What we think has a physical response, and what we eat, drink, and do (or don't do) has a direct effect on our brains. Our understanding of the brain-body relationship may indeed be the most exciting scientific advance of the 21st century. It is basic to the human experience and has largely been left on the shelf as a viable educational tool that enhances both teaching and learning.

HOW DOES THE BRAIN LEARN, AND HOW CAN MOVEMENT HELP THIS PROCESS BE MORE EFFICIENT?

The Learning Brain

The brain learns through the processing of sensory information from its surrounding environment. At the core of all this machinery, there are approximately 100 billion brain cells (neurons). Although neurons never actually touch, they form networks through chemical (neurotransmitter) transfers that consolidate information (see Figure 2.1 on page 18). When neurons communicate (Neuron A talks to Neuron B, B talks to C, and so on), you learn, process information, and form memory traces. If the memory trace is not lost through inactivity and rehearsal of new information takes place, more neurons are called on and a stronger alliance (neural network) is formed. When strong networks are formed, information from these neural communities is more easily retrieved.

Figure 2.1 Neuron Diagram

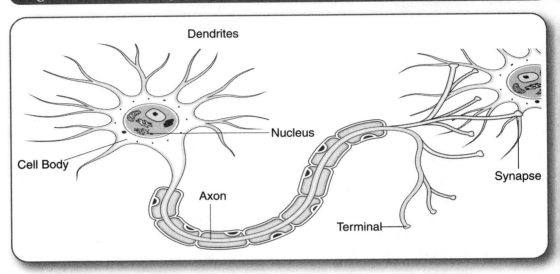

Learning and Memory

One goal of school learning is the memorization of large amounts of information. This does not happen without some difficulty because of the normal restraints of memory systems. Short-term memory is divided into immediate memory and working memory, both of which have very restrictive time and capacity limits (Sousa, 2006). The objective is for information to pass through both short-term memory components and move into long-term memory storage. This is easier said than done. Without a profound sense of interest or emotional connection, information can easily be forgotten. In other words, for information to move from working memory to long-term memory (the goal of school learning), something has to happen to the information or experience. Here are a few suggestions (Oberparleiter, 2004):

- Find a pattern
- Make connections
- Develop personal interest
- Associate it with prior experience
- Engage emotionally
- Practice it

In 1999, Marilee Sprenger, in her book *Learning and Memory: The Brain in Action*, proposed five different memory lanes through which the brain stores information in long-term memory. They are as follows:

1. Semantic—represents word meaning by using discussion and reading

2. Episodic—refers to location memory by creating pictures of where we were when an event occurred

3. Emotional—the most potent of all lanes, it processes emotionally charged events

4. Automatic—contains information that becomes automatic and readily available

5. Procedural—stores information related to movement

You might ask, is there an overlap between lanes? And the answer is yes. Identifying memory lanes simply helps us to quantify how and why memories are stored. What's interesting about automatic and procedural memory is that they are processed through the same part of the brain that coordinates movement: the cerebellum. Spending most of our time in the semantic memory lane limits access to powerful parts of the brain that may open new doors to learning. Old models of the cerebellum having to do with only movement have been replaced by new research and models that feature the cerebellum as an important support structure for emotions, memory, cognition, analysis, and decision making.

Movement Makes the Learning Process More Efficient

Through both an examination of an expansive body of literature on brain research and 35 years of public and private school instruction, educational consultant Lee Oberparleiter (2004) developed what he calls the 12 brain-compatible principles. Movement can play a direct role in five of those principles during the classroom experience:

1. *The brain is attracted to novelty.* The six purposes of movement can be used to provide this desired novelty.

2. *The brain pays attention to movement.* Movement with purpose acts to keep the attention and focus of students.

3. *The brain needs to interact with people and things in its environment.* Class cohesion activities using movement build a sense of community and interaction among classmates.

4. *Learning is easier to store, remember, and retrieve if it has an emotional base.* Movement activities often create positive emotional states causing students to link positive emotions with learning.

5. *The brain operates from concrete experience—everything stems from that.* Nothing is more concrete than using movement to learn or review a concept.

Using the six purposes of movement in the classroom is a brain-friendly endeavor that purposefully and carefully leads to lessons that engage the whole brain and all memory lanes. Therefore, *movement with purpose* becomes a viable and brain-friendly teaching tool. Here are some examples of how movement can make the learning process more efficient:

- Makes more pathways accessible to learning and memory than with a traditional model

- Involves more sensory engagement, making learning more accessible and paying attention easier
- Makes recall easier. Physical experiences are often much easier to recall than those that only engage the semantic memory (books and words) lane
- Engages whole-brain learning for a more clear and total picture of learning versus a traditional left-hemisphere (language-oriented) lesson
- Provides immediate rehearsal of new information, which is critical to learning and memory, and provides a multisensory opportunity for efficient learning, rehearsal, and storage of information
- Allows for an efficient means of doing something to the experience (reviewing or learning new content) that becomes a dynamic three-dimensional, rich sensory experience that creates transfer of information from immediate memory all the way to long-term memory storage

CAN PHYSICAL ACTIVITY, MOVEMENT, AND ACADEMICS BE COMBINED TO ENHANCE THE LEARNING PROCESS?

An Elementary Success Story: The Action Based Learning Lab (ABL)

The Action Based Learning Lab, developed by neurokinesiologist Jean Blaydes Madigan and retired physical education teacher Cindy Hess (2004), supports the link between physical activity and academic performance. Human technology allows students to be actively engaged as they jump rope, walk on specially designed rungs of a ladder, and perform many other physical tasks. While performing these movements, students also solve math problems, read word walls, and review and learn other essential content. In Ephrata, Pennsylvania, the Highland Elementary had fully embraced the lab. The result was only 4 students out of 220 not reading at grade level (kindergarten through second grade). The norm is approximately 12 to 15 not reading at grade level. The Prince William County (Virginia) Public Schools have also reported dramatic success in using the Action Based Learning Lab with first graders in need of intervention and remediation. The benefits of using movement in the classroom and the experiences students are getting from this program validate the science. The connection between physical activity and brain function is evident. In a world where technology seems to be outdated by the time you have had a morning cup of coffee, it is becoming clear that the greatest technological tool at our disposal is a comfortable pair of sneakers. Here are some key points of the Action Based Learning Lab (Blaydes Madigan, 1999):

- Brain science supports a strong link between movement and learning.
- The brain and body's movement and learning systems are interdependent and interactive.

- Motor development provides the framework that the brain uses to sequence the patterns needed for academic concepts.
- The body's vestibular system controls balance and spatial awareness and facilitates the student's ability to place words and letters on a page.
- The four visual fields needed for eye tracking are strengthened during many of the activities.
- The progressive stations prepare the brain for input and processing.
- Along with developing physical fitness, sensory components of balance, coordination, spatial awareness, directionality, and visual literacy are also developed. These components are developed as children roll, creep, crawl, spin, twirl, bounce, balance, walk, jump, juggle, and support their weight in space.
- Self-awareness, self-esteem, and social skills are also enhanced through the program.

Each progression and station allows the student to experience challenge, feedback, and physical activity. These three components are necessary for optimal learning.

Imagine visiting a classroom where students are joyfully engaged in schoolwork, discipline problems are nonexistent, and students are cooperative and encouraging one another. This would be educational utopia. The Action Based Learning Lab provides an atmosphere where students are not only reviewing and learning content, but also are building relationships and a love of learning and school. What other pedagogical methodology could possibly be meeting the needs of so many children at one time while creating an atmosphere of joyful learning and engagement? Physical activity and movement are the two key ingredients that give the Action Based Learning Lab its success. It is the ultimate application of the brain-body connection in an educational sense.

Elementary Success Story from Blaydes, J. 1999. *Thinking on Your Feet*. Murphy, Texas: Action Based Learning. Used with permission.

A Secondary Success Story: Learning Readiness PE (LRPE)

Another prime example of a program that uses the brain-body connection to improve the academic success of students is Learning Readiness PE. This program was designed by Paul Zientarski, along with other physical education teachers in the Naperville School District in Naperville, Illinois. This program was based on limited research that suggested students who are more physically active are more academically alert. These students have the potential for experiencing enhanced brain development and growth in brain cells. Here are some key points and results from the program (Ratey, 2008):

- Exercising the body will also exercise the brain.
- Students participating in the program have all experienced significant gains in their reading ability and comprehension as well as improvement in math and other courses.

- Starting their day with physical workouts seems to wake up students' brains while preparing them for upcoming classes.
- Initially, students voluntarily took the 7:00 a.m. physical education class before attending their regular reading and math classes. In one semester, those with LRPE improved their reading and comprehension scores by 0.5 grade levels more than those students in the study who took the literacy class alone. The results were just as compelling with the students who took LRPE before math class. These students increased their algebra readiness by an average of 20.4% compared to 3.87% in the students without LRPE. Currently, the program is mandatory.
- Stations include cardiovascular workouts, vocabulary and literacy games, core strength training, exercising while learning the content, juggling, tumbling, cross-lateral exercises, balancing activities, cup stacking, jumping rope, and Brain Age II (Nintendo software that forces the brain to do things quickly).

The success of this program has many educators excited! Movement and fitness appear to be directly connected with academic achievement. The physical education staff in the Naperville School District is showing the role that physical activity plays in improving test scores. They are also teaching life skills that promote healthy living. Students are learning to push themselves in the gymnasium as well as in the classroom. This program is opening doors to understanding the many benefits that movement provides the learning process.

HOW DOES ACTION RESEARCH SUPPORT MOVEMENT IN THE CLASSROOM?

Gratz College in Melrose Park, Pennsylvania, requires all masters of arts in education candidates to complete an intensive nine-credit action research project to graduate. This has resulted in thousands of action research designs and implementations over the past two decades that examine classroom pedagogical practice and enhances instruction across eastern Pennsylvania.

The class of 2009 produced 250 pieces of action research ranging from *The Effects of the Study Island Intervention Program on Comprehension, Interpretation and Literary Analysis* to *The Impact of Visual Media on Law and Government Seniors*. From the authors' perspectives, the most exciting research was done on using movement and kinesthetic activity in the classroom. No less than 17 action research designs were focused on the impact of movement on the teaching and learning process in such diverse settings and populations as high school Spanish, third through fifth grade learning support, and secondary students with traumatic brain injury.

The resulting research using movement in the classroom was strongly positive, which will hopefully lead to more inquiry in this largely untapped area of education. Nearly all studies commented on the positive effect of movement on motivation levels and the creation of a more enjoyable classroom environment. More specifically, Burr (2009) found a high correlation between kinesthetic activities and increased spelling assessment scores in the second-grade classroom. Gibbs (2009) identified improved comprehension and authentic use of Spanish in the high school Spanish classroom using bodily-kinesthetic activities. Harding (2009) cited a dramatic increase in all students in the degree of attending through performing gross motor activities before structured academic lessons in an early intervention program. Wood (2009) found that students were able to retain information in greater amounts and more easily if movement activities were used in lessons in the seventh-grade classroom. Adams (2009) found that kinesthetic activities helped raise benchmark scores, create class enthusiasm, and enhance the overall academic experience in the eighth-grade classroom. Hubbard (2009) discovered that using movement-oriented activities with students who had suffered traumatic brain injury created a positive impact on student understanding of number concepts and enabled them to compute simple addition problems more easily. Her research was some of the first of its kind.

Taken as a whole, the 17 action research projects (see Resources for projects not listed here) inform us that using movement and kinesthetic activities in various ways:

- Increases motivation levels
- Creates positive learning states and classroom environments
- Can raise test scores
- Prepares the brain and body for learning
- Increases levels of student participation, attention, and engagement
- Helps students to more easily retain and recall information

Although many more projects will be completed in the coming years, it is both exciting and gratifying to know what many intuitive teachers already know: Using movement in the classroom builds positive learning environments and increases student engagement and learning.

For more information on the Gratz College action research process or existing research on a diverse range of topics dealing with teaching and learning, please call 800–475–4635 extension 134.

WHAT ARE 10 CRITICAL REASONS WHY EDUCATORS SHOULD USE THE SIX PURPOSES OF MOVEMENT TO IMPROVE LEARNING?

Reason 1: Movement Provides a Break From Learning and Refocuses Attention

Working memory, whose activity mostly occurs in the frontal lobe, has capacity limits especially when dealing with new information that has no relevance to the learner. The hippocampus, crucial to the conversion of working memory to long-term memory, has a limited capacity and can be easily overwhelmed. Imagine this part of the brain being the size of a paper cup. Teachers often try to fill this paper cup with information that would fit into a large pitcher! As far as learning and the brain are concerned, shorter is usually better. Built in brain breaks (Purpose 2) and time for processing academic content are essential to the learning process. Movement can provide a necessary break from learning and actually make the entire process more efficient.

Refocusing attention may just be the most useful benefit of movement. Some have referred to the power of movement to refocus students as "magical." Upon finishing movement activities with teachers and/or students, it is normal for them to feel more focused and attentive. It's simply working with the brain instead of against it. Using Purpose 3 (supporting exercise and fitness), an educator can refocus his or her students' attention in seconds. For example, asking students to stand and perform 10 jumping jacks is a quick way to give the brain a burst of fresh oxygen while refocusing it for further learning.

Remember, students are always paying attention, probably just not to the teacher. Don't be offended, it's just a survival mechanism of the brain. Every teacher in a classroom and every administrator in a meeting has witnessed yawning, glazed-over eyes, and staring out the window. As previously described, using movement can be a quick and easy way to bring someone's focus and attention back where it belongs. This is especially important for students dealing with attention deficit disorder (ADD) and attention deficit hyperactivity disorder (ADHD). Research suggests that a lack of movement can cause or contribute to the symptoms of hyperactivity. Children with hyperactivity disorders who run before class have shown significant behavior improvement to the point of having their medication reduced if running occurred on a daily basis (Putnam, 2003).

Reason 2: Movement Allows for Implicit Learning

Implicit learning is generally defined as learning that takes place beyond our conscious awareness. Though there are many ways for this to take place, movement is a strong implicit learning tool. Much of school learning occurs explicitly through reading, listening, discussion, worksheets, lectures, and the memorization of rote material that is often beyond the learner's realm of relevance and interest. Students spend much of their school day learning through explicit channels, yet it is not the brain's preferred way of learning nor is it the most efficient. Brain research over the past two decades has provided a more precise window into the world of how we learn and has shed light on the power of implicit learning and its implications for the classroom. This does not mean that explicit and implicit learning are mutually exclusive. There is overlap, as they work to support each other. A blurred line exists where one ends and the other begins in the learning process. Still, the brain naturally learns through implicit channels driven by emotion and movement and characterized by both procedural (riding a bike) learning powered by the cerebellum and reflexive (emotional) learning processed through the amygdala (see Figure 2.2). It is interesting to note that the cerebellum, once thought to play a role in only coordinating movement, also takes part in matters of attention, long-term memory, spatial perception, impulse control, and other

Figure 2.2 Brain Diagram

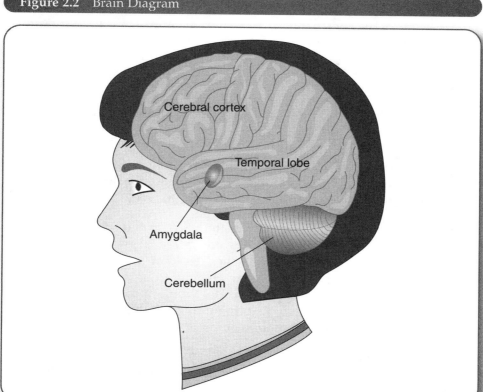

cognitive functions. Movement plays a critical role in learning and memory. Using the six purposes of movement will increase the amount of implicit learning in the classroom.

Reason 3: Movement Improves Brain Function

What is good for the heart is good for the brain. Movement in the form of prolonged aerobic exercise not only enhances cognitive function and memory but also helps create an environment where new brain cells can grow and thrive. Not long ago, this process, known as neurogenesis, was thought impossible. Dr. Ratey (2008) has helped usher in a new era of popular understanding of what it means to move and what it means for brain-body health. He emphasizes a perspective of the brain being the primary recipient of the benefits of aerobic exercise. The cardiovascular and musculoskeletal benefits then become a very desirable by-product. Ratey states that exercise (Purpose 3) enhances learning by:

- Improving attention while increasing alertness and motivation
- Encouraging nerve cells to bond to one another, which is the basis for new learning
- Promoting neurogenesis, which is the development of new nerve cells

Reason 4: Movement Meets Basic Needs

As a part of his choice theory and internal control psychology, William Glasser (1998) identifies the following as basic human needs:

- Survival
- Belonging
- Power
- Freedom
- Fun

These needs are often not addressed in a school setting causing behavior and academic problems as well as frustration for teachers and students. In *Activating the Desire to Learn*, author Bob Sullo (2007) writes:

> The good news is that we can create learning environments that foster the motivation that makes education a joyful enterprise. Internal control psychology teaches us that we are driven to connect, to be competent, to make choices, to have fun, and to be safe. Structure a classroom and school where those five needs are regularly met, and you will inspire motivation that fuels academic excellence and exemplary behavior.

Implementing the six purposes of movement can do just that. Building kinesthetic classrooms while creating optimal learning states is an inexpensive, simple, and accessible way for teachers to meet student needs. When students are allowed to engage in the learning process through movement, both the survival and freedom needs are met through supporting brain function and allowing students to move throughout the room. The need for power is met through enhanced competence because of matched learning style and more accessibility to content. Implicit learning, which represents differentiation by learning profile, is utilized, thus reaching far more learners than with a traditional model. Movement-oriented classroom cohesion activities build belonging and trust, which is essential to creating a sustainable home for the brain. Finally, when the decision is made to use more movement in the classroom, the learning and environment become fun. In turn, students want to take part in learning instead of feeling disengaged. The kinesthetic classroom just might be the most profound classroom learning strategy available to teachers to meet basic needs.

Innovation is always in great demand in the classroom. An understanding of the brain-body connection is critical for teachers to be effective designers of the learning environment. The kinesthetic classroom puts simple brain-body technologies to use and enhances the schooling experience for both teacher and student.

Reason 5: Movement Improves the Learning State

The management of students' learning states is often an unfamiliar concept to teachers. This notion plays an important role in the success that teachers have in reaching and educating their students. At the end of the day, the learning process comes down to the interaction between student and teacher. That interaction becomes effective when teachers can manage students' learning states successfully. The ultimate goal is for students to develop the ability to self-regulate and manage their learning states. This would include keeping focused as their attention begins to drift while maintaining a positive state of mind. For example, when sitting for a 45-minute lecture on a given topic, it is only natural for the mind to wander. Compared to students, adults are more likely to control their state of mind by doing little things that help them to stay focused and attentive. They may say mental reminders, chew gum, take notes, or do something that has helped them to stay focused and constructive in the past. Students are typically lacking this skill and must learn it over time.

Eric Jensen (2000) tells us that a student's learning state has a great influence on the meaning that is created during the learning process. He says that meaning making is state dependent (see Figure 2.3). Therefore, if a student has a positive learning state when material is being taught, the student has a better opportunity to make connections and understand the concepts and the information they are learning. Sousa (2006) indicates that meaning and sense are two nonnegotiable criteria for content retention. Of the two, meaning is more potent. As mentioned previously, movement is the most powerful manager of students' learning states (Jensen). Educators who use the six purposes of movement will have a well-balanced, effective means of managing student learning states. This will allow for improved academic success for many students.

Figure 2.3   Movement, State Management, and Meaning

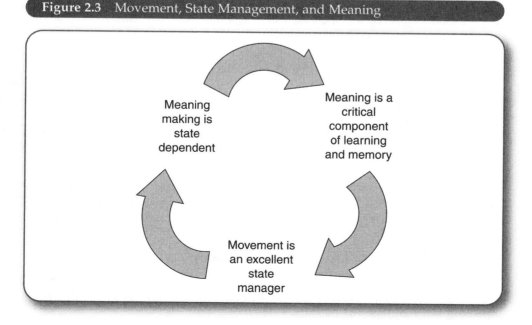

Reason 6: Movement Differentiates Instruction

Modern classrooms are characterized by the uniqueness and diversity of learners. Differentiating by learning style then becomes an essential teaching tool. It has been suggested that 85% of students are predominately kinesthetic learners, which means that they rely on kinesthetic intelligence for learning. In other words, these children prefer to move their bodies while participating in the learning process. As a response to this high percentage, it is essential that educators incorporate movement in their classroom. If most school learning depends on speaking and listening skills, then we are not doing justice to the students that prefer to learn kinesthetically. An effective way to reach these learners would simply be to implement the six purposes of movement in the classroom. By teaching content through movement (Purpose 6), educators differentiate instruction to meet the needs of the kinesthetic learner. This provides an atmosphere of challenge, acceptance, and achievement.

Reason 7: Movement Engages the Senses

The brain learns and stores information through sensory cues. The more senses used for learning, the more likely the information will be learned and stored. In a classroom setting, this often happens through listening, writing, seeing, and discussing. Adding the six purposes of movement to the curriculum, or as a support to the curriculum, increases the likelihood that information will be learned, stored, and more easily retrieved for later use and transfer. Rarely do students have the opportunity to experience content though movement and the use of their body. Of all sensory information, sight, hearing, and touch (including kinesthetic experiences) contribute most to our learning (Sousa, 2006). Education is often missing the kinesthetic piece. For information to be stored, something has to happen to it via sensory input. Learning through kinesthetic means can provide a very strong link to content and its retention and retrieval.

Reason 8: Movement Reduces Stress

Schools and classrooms are stressful environments (Queen & Queen, 2004). These stressors come from many areas, including prolonged sitting, academic expectations, disconnect feelings from the school setting, social and peer pressure, and unmet needs. Movement and exercise can have a positive effect on the brain as it aides in the reduction of stress levels. The use of the six purposes of movement as a part of an integrated classroom experience can serve to foster a positive classroom climate. This can result in an environment that minimizes stress while maximizing learning.

Reason 9: Movement Increases Circulation

Sitting for long periods causes blood to pool in the buttocks and legs, which means less blood is getting to the brain. This results in an undesirable learning state. Simply allowing students to stand up and move around while incorporating the six purposes of movement alleviates these issues by increasing heart rate and blood flow to the brain. Getting fresh oxygen to the brain will create a more effective learning state.

Reason 10: Movement Enhances Episodic Learning and Memory

During a learning episode, an environmental address is created in connection with the data. In other words, the brain makes note of where it is when it learns something. When movement is used to learn a concept, a unique environmental note is made by the brain making the information easier to recall. Through the six purposes of movement, it is possible for the brain to create unique environmental pictures of learning, which can enhance students' ability to recall information later.

Chapter 2 Recap

- Each year brings new evidence supporting the notion that the brain and body have been mistakenly assumed separate entities when, in fact, they flow to and through each other: both an extension and reflection of the other's will.
- The Action Based Learning Lab (elementary success story) and Learning Readiness PE (secondary success story) are programs that are finding an improvement in academic success by combining movement with academic content.
- There are 10 critical reasons the purposes of movement should be used to enhance learning.

  o Reason 1: Movement provides a break from learning and refocuses attention.
  o Reason 2: Movement allows for implicit learning.
  o Reason 3: Movement improves brain function.
  o Reason 4: Movement meets basic needs.
  o Reason 5: Movement improves the learning state.
  o Reason 6: Movement differentiates instruction.
  o Reason 7: Movement engages the senses.
  o Reason 8: Movement reduces stress.
  o Reason 9: Movement increases circulation.
  o Reason 10: Movement enhances episodic learning and memory.

3

Classroom Management

⇨ Will students be motivated to participate in movement activities in a classroom setting?

⇨ How can I manage students during movement activities?

⇨ How do I manage the unmotivated student during movement?

⇨ How do I manage the hypermotivated student during movement?

⇨ How can I maintain a safe environment and have an efficient transition from activity to seat?

WILL STUDENTS BE MOTIVATED TO PARTICIPATE IN MOVEMENT ACTIVITIES IN A CLASSROOM SETTING?

Some teachers and administrators might feel that using movement in the classroom could lead to discipline problems and lack of control. Although this is a possibility, it is no more likely than problems occurring with any other instructive methodology. In fact, when used purposefully and carefully, movement can lead to a more focused, productive, and disciplined classroom. This book describes the philosophy of *controlled movement with purpose*. When behaviors are managed and students are learning through movement with a distinct goal in mind, the teacher has control! This chapter will focus on tips for managing behavior while using the six purposes of movement.

In any given classroom, there are many different personality types and learning styles. Initially, some students might not choose movement or kinesthetic activities as their preference for learning in an academic setting. However, common sense and research inform us that most students do not prefer to sit and listen all day. The concept of movement in a classroom might still be new to many students, as physical activity might remind them of physical education. It becomes the teacher's responsibility to convince students that movement belongs in a classroom setting as well as in a gymnasium. This means providing preliminary information and motivation so students have an interest in participating in movement activities in an academic setting. This can be accomplished by explaining the six purposes of movement and how they can be used to improve academic success.

It is important to point out that from a physiological standpoint all bodies are designed to move. The body has obvious, positive responses to movement. When engaged in physical activity, people of all ages, typically, experience pleasure. As a result of movement, the brain releases neurotransmitters (such as serotonin and dopamine) and hormones (such as endorphins and adrenaline), all of which promote pleasure and excitement. Therefore, students will typically be motivated to move in a classroom setting.

What do I do with students who show resistance? This is something teachers need to be prepared to face. An initial consideration in these situations is to try to identify the reason or cause for the lack of motivation for each particular student. Listed next are five reasons why students may not be motivated to move.

1. Poor self-perception
   o Students with low self-esteem avoid movement activities because they feel they will not be successful.
   o Students with low self-esteem may often refuse to participate in physical activity rather than take the chance of potentially failing and/or looking foolish.
   o Students with low self-esteem may feel intimidated by movement and physical activity, especially if they view their skill level as poor.
   o Teacher tip: Creating a positive environment with movement will be essential to build this particular student's motivation.

2. Negative or limited past experiences
   o Students may be fearful of movement when they have limited experiences because they are unfamiliar with the joy that it brings.
   o Students may mentally revisit unpleasant past experiences with physical activity as they try to avoid it.
   o These students tend to feel inferior as they engage in activities. They often create reasons for why they are unable to participate.

○ Teacher tip: Starting with simple activities that lead to immediate success will be very important to these students. Patience and ample positive feedback are key factors.

3. Low and/or unclear expectations in the classroom

○ Students often rise to meet teacher expectations.
○ Students are more likely to trust themselves and their abilities while engaging in physical activities if teachers believe that students can learn through movement.
○ Challenge students by providing an environment that motivates the learners to give their best while participating in activities.
○ Teacher tip: Believe that your students are able to show success in movement activities, and create an environment that encourages participation. Make a connection between effort and achievement.

4. Feeling pressure

○ Students often respond negatively to pressure and may refuse to participate in activities.
○ These students may often act out or isolate themselves during movement because they are concerned with how others will view them.
○ They may display an "I don't care" attitude, as they struggle to deal with their perceived stress.
○ Teacher tip: Provide a supportive, stress-free experience with movement so students feel accepted.

5. Limited support in the home or family environment

○ Students' initial beliefs about movement may be influenced by attitudes at home.
○ In a home where physical activity is encouraged, children are given an important message about the benefits of movement and are more likely to face the movement challenges that teachers provide.
○ In a home where physical activity is not encouraged, children are given the message that movement is insignificant.
○ Teacher tip: Be patient as you expose students to a new way of looking at movement. Develop an understanding of why these students show resistance.

HOW CAN I MANAGE STUDENTS DURING MOVEMENT ACTIVITIES?

Diverse viewpoints exist about what strategies yield success when it comes to classroom management. All teachers go through a period of trial and error to develop various strategies to employ with different personality types in their classroom. Educators also need to take into consideration their own character. When it comes to classroom management during movement activities, these same rules apply. Careful preparation is needed to handle students who are both unmotivated and hypermotivated. Patience is required, as it may take time to find one's comfort level. Effective management strategies will develop along the way.

The first consideration regarding classroom management and movement is prevention. Try to visualize your students participating in movement activities, and ask, "What potential problems could arise?" Consider students that will challenge you or the activity. Is there any strategy or technique you can use to prevent problems before they begin? Mentally going through the steps and rules of any activity numerous times is a critical step in preventing problems and ensuring success. Also, keep in mind that you will face situations and activities that simply fail. It is impossible to get everything right, every time. Effective management of student behavior during movement activities is a skill that develops as you continue to experiment with various methods. Here are 11 classroom-management techniques to consider prior to getting started.

1. Define expectations
   - Let students know you expect them to act appropriately while participating.
   - List and discuss the consequences for students' misbehavior during movement activities.
   - Be very clear. This is one of the most important steps because it will set students up for success.

2. Prepare the room
   - Establish a routine for preparing a large space in the classroom (e.g., putting all the desks to the sides or back of the room and getting them back in place). A horseshoe configuration can make this process very easy.
   - Have students practice the procedure so they can prepare for movement activities in less than two minutes.

3. Use basic cues
   - Keep cues simple and clear.
   - Using a whistle is an effective means for getting students' attention immediately.

4. Use partners effectively
   - Partners can be assigned, students can be allowed to choose their partner, or you can use creative ways to make partners. Certain classes may have more difficulty picking their partners, so consider what will work best for your given situation.

- ○ Students should work productively with their partners.
- ○ If students are not working well together, change partners and reconsider your method for choosing partners.

5. Provide time limits

- ○ Keep students on task during movement activities by setting time limits.
- ○ Set all limits with expectations and consequences.

6. Repeat the objectives for the activity

- ○ Off-task students may be testing you.
- ○ React quickly and follow through with previously stated consequences.
- ○ If too many students are off task, you need to revisit the rules of the activity and the goals of the lesson.

7. Start small

- ○ Doing something small in the front of the room, such as throwing a ball to students who are raising their hand or using quick brain breaks, is a simple and effective way to begin to use movement in a classroom.
- ○ Activities that are performed alone or with one partner are also simple ways to start.
- ○ Refrain from engaging students in large-group activities until a comfort level is established.

8. Be firm

- ○ Do not allow students to participate if they are off task and disruptive.
- ○ Movement activities must be taken seriously because of the safety factor (unless, of course, you are doing a silly class cohesion activity or a brain break).
- ○ Set the standards for your high expectations right from the beginning of the year and before activities.
- ○ Being firm does not mean that you need to be loud and intimidating.
- ○ Respond quietly and swiftly to situations so problems do not escalate.

9. Prepare a step-by-step approach

- ○ Know how you will present the material, game, or activity beforehand.
- ○ Be proactive and try to prevent negative situations from occurring.
- ○ Practice responding to different behavioral challenges so you will know what to do if they do occur.

10. Controlled/directed and safe movements first

    ○ Begin with movements that have specific directions before heading toward more creative movements.
    ○ Begin with movements that won't embarrass students.

11. Move continuously

    ○ Move around the room during movement activities.
    ○ Let students know you are watching.

HOW DO I MANAGE THE UNMOTIVATED STUDENT DURING MOVEMENT?

The Elementary Student

Most elementary students love and need to move. Generally, young children will move their bodies whether you want them to or not. Therefore, it is essential to consider the six purposes of movement. If students are going to move, despite the wishes of the teacher, it only makes sense that they move their bodies with a teacher-directed goal in mind. If an elementary student is struggling to sit still, the result may be poor behavior, and students may begin to act out. However, if students are moving to learn, which comes naturally, classroom management will be easier. Through movement, an environment is being created that meets students' basic needs, and the result will be a better-managed classroom.

What should you do if an elementary student is unmotivated or refusing to participate in movement activities? Once again, a trial-and-error phase must happen for each teacher. There is not one clear answer, but many solutions, responses, and/or reactions work. These strategies will be discussed throughout this chapter.

The Secondary Student

It is likely that some secondary students will show an initial resistance toward movement. Students have linked learning academic content to sitting in a chair for many years. There may be an adjustment period, which requires your patience and understanding. Although the unmotivated child at the secondary level is common, with a few tips and strategies, the secondary educator will be prepared to handle these students effectively.

The way movement activities are presented to these students will play a key role in how they respond. Being willing to try new things and keeping students on their toes can quickly earn you respect. This respect can be a preliminary motivator for older students. By allowing your excitement and support for learning through movement to shine, students will respond with curiosity and interest. For the students who do not show interest, you must be prepared to respond swiftly to any given behavior.

Listed next are several points to take into account when considering effective strategies for managing unmotivated students during movement activities. The following seven ideas should prove useful to both elementary and secondary teachers.

1. Use rewards carefully

   o Movement is the reward.
   o Students who are intrinsically motivated will be more willing to face movement challenges because of how it makes them feel.
   o Students who are extrinsically motivated participate to gain a reward, avoid a punishment, or gain attention. This may lead to limited effort from the student.
   o Teaching and learning through movement is a great example of intrinsic motivation.

2. Avoid power struggles

   o Set clear expectations and consequences for all movement activities.
   o If you need to act, be reasonable, calm, and consistent.
   o Consequences should be fair and effective.
   o If a student refuses to participate in an activity, be prepared with an alternative activity. This is extremely important at the secondary level.
   o Allow students the choice to learn new academic concepts through movement or other means.
   o Students who initially choose the alternative means of learning will see others participating in the movement activities having fun and will most likely want to join.
   o Use contracts stating that students will participate in so many movement activities during a marking period.
   o Use scoring rubrics that incorporate a participation grade for movement.

3. Build on students' strengths

   o Find an area where your students excel. Focus on activities that will lead to feelings of success.
   o Constant failure can cause a lack of motivation during movement. Therefore, self-esteem and motivation will be lowered and students will be less willing to participate.
   o If students can find success in movement activities, determine the elements of that accomplishment.
   o Encourage students to high five one another after every movement activity.
   o Compliment positive peer interactions during physical activity and explain its importance.

4. Provide a secure environment

- Students need to feel that you value movement.
- If you demonstrate that movement is beneficial to learning, students will be more likely to develop similar attitudes.
- Allow your students to know that failure is a part of the learning process and allow them such without punishment or negativity.
- Students who are not afraid to fail are more willing to accept challenges and less likely to sabotage their efforts.
- Use activities where everyone wins when they try their best.

5. Take ownership

- Allow students the opportunity to feel they are an important part of all movement activities that happen in your classroom.
- Students who feel that their role of importance is equal to their peers' may be more willing to participate.

6. Set your expectations high

- Expect your students to participate in movement activities while following directions and staying on task.
- Movement is not an opportunity for students to lose control and do whatever they want.
- Movement provides the opportunity for controlled movement with purpose.

7. Encourage cooperation

- Ask students to help and compliment one another while providing positive feedback when appropriate.
- Students may become more motivated during movement activities when they feel they are part of a team.
- Foster positive talk and make your classroom a "team zone" where put-downs are forbidden.

Students lacking motivation want to succeed, but they are held back by some obstacle. With patience, understanding, and hard work, you can help all students find a path to achievement and an appreciation for movement. The unmotivated student can learn to love the six purposes of movement to the point of asking, "When can we move?"

HOW DO I MANAGE THE HYPERMOTIVATED STUDENT DURING MOVEMENT?

The Elementary Student

It is very common to encounter a hypermotivated student in an elementary classroom setting. Educators often have the challenge of managing this behavior on a daily basis. In many situations, movement and physical activity are exactly what the hypermotivated student needs. It is often difficult for this particular child to refrain from moving. They just need it! Encouraging hypermotivated students in organized movement activities allows these children the chance to do something their brain and body desire.

Many strategies can be used to manage the hypermotivated student during movement activities in an academic setting. The safety of all participants must be the number one concern at all times. Students who are hypermotivated can quickly lose control of their actions and become a danger to others. These students will require more visual attention. Responding to these students quickly and accurately will be very important in managing their behavior. Strategies to consider when managing the hypermotivated student will follow.

The Secondary Student

Dealing with a hypermotivated student at the secondary level will characteristically be infrequent. As students mature, some appear to become lethargic and inactive. However, some situations will dictate management of hypermotivated student at the secondary level. Once more, safety is the top priority. Precise responses to these students will be essential to maintaining class control.

Numerous approaches must be considered when dealing with the hypermotivated students during movement. If not handled correctly, these students can destroy the movement experience for everyone. They can be intimidating to others while their actions may be a complete distraction to the lesson objectives. Diligence is a key factor when managing the hypermotivated student during physical activity. Here are 10 considerations about managing the hypermotivated student at both the elementary and secondary levels.

1. Introduce material observantly
   o Because hypermotivated students' minds tend to wander, they often miss the directions. Make sure you have students' attention when giving directions for a movement activity.
   o Directions must be clear and precise.
   o Proximity can be effective in this situation.

2. Repeat Directions
   o Hypermotivated students typically need to hear the directions more than once.
   o Check for understanding before the movement begins.

3. State consequences consistently
   o List consequences for the students who are often off task and/or out of control during movement activities before you begin.

4. Respond immediately

 o If a student is off task and/or out of control, use the immediate consequence that was previously stated.
 o Once again, body control is especially important for individual and classroom safety.

5. Be consistent and fair

 o Follow through when reacting immediately to behavior problems during a movement activity.
 o Giving an off-task student wiggle room will signal others to move off task.

6. Avoid power struggles

 o Do not argue with the student.
 o Speak softly and give firm directions about what you want to see happen during the movement activity.

7. Avoid giving attention

 o Be careful not to give too much attention to hypermotivated students.
 o React immediately and appropriately, and then move on.
 o Quietly remove the student from the activity when necessary.
 o A break from the activity is sometimes crucial for maintaining safety and control.
 o Breaks do not have to be permanent; they can be short and effective while sending a clear message to other students.

8. Provide feedback

 o At the appropriate time, discuss the student's behavior.
 o Ask children to explain why they received the consequence.

9. Short- and long-term goals

 o Set goals for changing behavior for following movement activities.
 o Discuss different ways students can control themselves.

10. Prevention

 o Use strategies, such as allowing students to model correct play/ actions for movement activities while they contribute to the creation of rules and consequences.

Striving for controlled movement with purpose will yield success. This goal is reasonable and attainable. Through trial and error, effective means for managing behavior in your classroom during movement activities will be developed. The unmotivated and hypermotivated students will both challenge and strengthen you in many ways. This learning experience will build class cohesion, as your students begin to enjoy your lessons on a level not previously experienced. Students' motivation will grow as they look forward to entering your room, wondering what they will be doing next. As they leave your room for the day, they will already be anticipating tomorrow.

HOW CAN I MAINTAIN A SAFE ENVIRONMENT AND ASSURE AN EFFICIENT TRANSITION FROM ACTIVITY TO SEAT?

Safety

As mentioned previously, the highest priority when moving students in the classroom is safety. Two questions should be carefully considered. The first is, what rules must I enforce to maintain a safe environment for my students? The second is, how can I allow students to move around my classroom and still keep the equipment and physical objects from being broken or damaged? Contemplating these two concerns is crucial for success. While focusing on the safety of all students, the educator should ponder a few questions:

- What are my students wearing?
- What type of shoes do they have on their feet?
- Do my students vary in shape and size?
- Is jewelry a concern during this activity?

These areas allow very little control. However, the attire of your students must be considered when deciding whether they can participate in the activity. There is a potential solution to this concern. If students are moving on a daily basis, they will know what to expect in your classroom. Therefore, routines can be established where students come to class prepared with safe clothing and footwear. Removing jewelry takes minimal effort for the student.

What about students of different shapes and sizes? A possible solution is to have students take a driving test in your classroom. A driving test is practical for students of all ages and can prove that everyone can move safely in a given space. The driving test is as follows:

- Students imagine their bodies are cars.
- In a given space, they can choose their speed and direction for one minute as they move around the room.
- Some students will move quickly while others will drive more conservatively.
- Students must problem solve by analyzing the size of the space while considering the number of classmates in the space.
- If a car (body) gets in an accident with another car or an object in the room, the car must be parked for driving out of control.

- Younger children can receive basic directions for this test while older students can be addressed with instructions that are more elaborate.
- It is also essential to explain that sometimes people get in accidents even when they have their cars under control (e.g., two cars gently backing into each other with no damage versus someone crashing into another driver because they are on a cell phone, resulting in significant damage to both cars).
- The driving test gives the teacher a perfect opportunity to discuss noise level during movement activities, as students need to keep their horns (mouth) quiet.

This test is one example of how students can prove to both you and themselves that movement can be safe and fun in a classroom setting, as long as they keeps their bodies under control. In situations where there is little control, a quick response is needed through immediate consequence.

Considering the safety of the equipment and physical objects in your room is also important. Classroom environments can be a safe place for movement, but a room scan must be performed first. Here are some things to look for:

- What is breakable?
- Where are sharp objects or jagged corners located?
- Are there any areas on the floor that may cause students to trip?
- Is ceiling height a concern?
- How can I protect objects in my room?

Many steps can be taken to protect a classroom environment once a room scan is complete. The setup of your room, such as desks, computers, and chairs, can strategically be designed for student and environmental safety.

Transition Time

As the six purposes of movement are implemented, it is reasonable to be concerned about the amount of time it will take for students to quiet down once they have completed a movement activity. As previously discussed, physical activity will energize the body and brain. It may be challenging for students to go from invigorating activities to complete silence while sitting back in their chair. Patience is key, as students may require a minimal amount of transition time. The key word is "minimal." It is important for transition time to be efficient so very little time is lost. The most effective way to minimize transition time is to have a routine that is well established and understood by your students. Some methods for regaining students' attention are as follows:

- Waiting patiently in front of the room
- Moving to the center of the room and saying, "If you can hear me clap once," "If you can hear me clap twice."

- Using a bell or a distinct sound
- Placing a timer on an overhead and setting a goal of one minute for complete silence
- Raising your hand high in the air and asking students to follow (hand goes up, mouth goes closed)
- Turning out the lights
- Using a creative song or rhythmic clap

Find something that works for you, and explain the importance of efficient transition time to your students. Once a routine is established, allow students time to practice and master the skill. This will play an important role in classroom management. Remember to keep your routine clear, simple, and consistent.

Chapter 3 Recap

- Controlled movement with purpose can be used to manage classroom behaviors during movement activities.

- Identification of unmotivated students is critical. Lack of motivation may be caused by low self-esteem, negative or limited past experiences, low expectations in the classroom, pressure, and lack of support at home.

- Classroom-management strategies and tips are the following: define expectations, prepare the room, use cues, practice preparing a space for movement, use a variety of ways to make partners, set time limits, reemphasize objectives, start small, be firm, come down hard early, visualize a step-by-step approach, move around the room, and use safe and directed movements first.

- Educators should consider the following ideas when managing unmotivated students during movement activities: use rewards carefully, avoid power struggles, build on students' strengths, provide an encouraging/secure environment, allow students to take ownership, set your expectations high, and encourage cooperation.

- Educators should consider the following ideas when managing hypermotivated students during movement activities: clearly introduce material, repeat directions, maintain high expectations, list consequences, react immediately, be consistent, avoid power struggles and giving attention, give feedback, set goals, and focus on preventing problems before they occur.

- The educator must go through a trial-and-error process to discover which classroom strategies will work best for them. Controlled movement with purpose is attainable and may result in an exciting, desirable classroom setting.

- Always consider the safety of your students and the equipment and/or physical objects in your classroom.

- Establish an efficient routine for transitioning students from movement activities back to a seated position.

Preparing the Brain

> ⇨ When should brain-compatible movements be used to prepare the brain for learning? Should I link them to academic content?
>
> ⇨ What are 10 movement activities that cross the midline of the body and improve visual tracking?
>
> ⇨ What are 18 movement activities that develop the vestibular system and spatial awareness?

WHEN SHOULD BRAIN-COMPATIBLE MOVEMENTS BE USED TO PREPARE THE BRAIN FOR LEARNING? SHOULD I LINK THEM TO ACADEMIC CONTENT?

The activities in this chapter are appropriate for most grade, fitness, and ability levels. These movements can be implemented in a one- to three-minute timeframe throughout your lessons. When deciding how to implement them, consider your objective. For example, if you are asking students to read and/or write, it is reasonable to engage students in brain-compatible movement activities that cross the midline of the body. Both hemispheres of the brain are involved with reading and writing. Your goal is to get both sides of the brain communicating, to achieve greater success with the presented challenge. To help improve visual tracking, encourage students to follow their body parts with their eyes. Students can also participate in activities that develop the vestibular system to better track words on a page. If these activities do not work for all students, they, at least, serve as a brief break from academic content.

These fun, simple movements are easy to incorporate. Look for windows that present an ideal opportunity to prepare the brain for learning. Here are a few to consider:

- At the start of the day
- Before diving into an academic goal
- Between academic activities
- When students show signs of boredom
- When students appear restless
- Before, during, and after testing
- While teaching and reviewing your academic content

Anchoring content with movement combines academic pursuits and kinesthetic activities, which has shown to increase test scores in elementary students (Blaydes Madigan & Hess, 2004). Creative thought in the design of these activities will enhance the entire process. Academic content and specific movements can be combined in many ways. For instance, students can do the following:

- Perform heel taps or windmills while reciting the alphabet.
- Juggle one or two scarves while counting odd and even numbers.
- Spin 360 degrees while understanding the planets and the solar system.
- Point to designated places on a map while holding a balance pose.
- Leap frog to the points on a geometric shape.
- Jump rope while reading a word wall.

Allowing children to participate in movements that facilitate learning should prove beneficial. At the very least, these activities serve to reenergize learners as they pursue academic goals and standards.

WHAT ARE 10 MOVEMENT ACTIVITIES THAT CROSS THE MIDLINE OF THE BODY AND IMPROVE VISUAL TRACKING?

Full Body Crossing

1. Grapevine
   - This is a lateral movement where students will face forward as they move sideways.
   - Students will take their right foot and step to the right.
   - They will then step with their left foot and cross it over the front of the right.
   - The next step will be the right foot out to the side followed by the left foot crossing behind the right.

- Continue this pattern of step, cross in front, step, cross behind, step, cross in front, and so on.
- The pattern can also begin by going the opposite direction or by facing the other way and stepping to the left (the right would then cross in front).

2. Heel taps

- Have students stand with their feet shoulder width apart and hands by their sides.
- Students will bend their left knee so the heel of the foot is just above the right knee.
- They will tap the left heel with their right hand.
- They will then bend the left knee in the opposite direction so their heel is pointing toward their buttocks.
- They will tap the heel with their right hand.
- Have students switch sides.
- Bend the right knee so that it is just above the left knee and tap it with the left hand.
- Then bend the right knee in the opposite direction toward the buttocks and tap it with the left hand.
- Have students continue varying speeds.

 **Figure 4.1**   Heel Taps

3. Windmills

- o Have students stand with their feet wide apart and their arms reaching out to the sides.
- o Students will swing their right hand down to touch their left toes or ankle (straight legs or a slight bend in the knees is appropriate).
- o Stand up and swing the left hand down to the right toes or ankle.
- o Continue varying speeds.

4. Hand clapping—toe tapping

- o Have students stand with feet shoulder width apart and arms reaching out to their sides.
- o Cross the right foot in front of the left leg and tap the toe to the ground. At the same time, cross the right arm over the body and clap with the left hand.
- o Go back to the beginning position.
- o Now, cross the left foot in front of the right leg and tap the toe to the ground. At the same time, cross the left arm over the body and clap with the right hand.
- o Go back to the beginning position and continue the pattern.

Figure 4.2   Hand Clapping—Toe Tapping

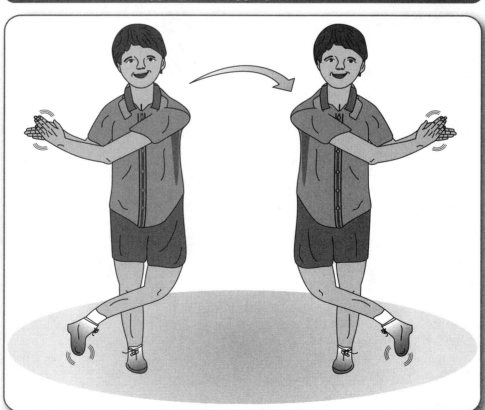

5. Head—shoulder—knees—toes
   o Have students cross their arms and bend their elbows so they are touching their right ear with their left hand and their left ear with their right hand.
   o Now, they will uncross their hands and move them to their shoulders.
   o Cross arms and go to the knees; uncross and go to the toes.
   o Continue with head, shoulders, knees, and toes while varying speeds and alternating crossed and uncrossed arms. (Have students change the order—toes, knees, shoulders, head.)

6. Body taps
   o Have students cross the midline of their body while tapping the following body parts: right fingers to left ear; right hand to left shoulder, elbow, and wrist; right elbow to left knee; right hand to left foot.
   o Allow students to switch and cross to the other side—left crossing over to right.
   o You can have students tap the same body part while alternating sides for a designated time or repetitions (e.g., 15 shoulder, elbow, and wrist taps per side).

Progressive Juggling

7. Juggling with one scarf
   o Give each student one juggling scarf.
   o Ask students to place the scarf in their right hand.
   o Students will throw the scarf up in the air to the left side of their body.
   o Be sure the right hand crosses the midline of the body.
   o Students will catch the scarf with their left hand.
   o They will then throw the scarf up in the air to the right side of their body (crossing the midline).
   o Students will catch the scarf with their right hand.
   o Continue while increasing speed.
   o You can also have students add a spin in this activity: Throw the scarf with the right hand to the left side of the body, spin to the right 360 degrees, and catch the scarf with the left hand.

8. Juggling with two scarves
   o Give each student two juggling scarves (one in each hand).
   o Students will throw the right scarf in the air toward their left side of their body. Immediately after the first toss, the scarf in the left hand is thrown to the right side of the body.
   o Both hands must cross the midline of the body.
   o To catch the scarves, the hands become uncrossed. Therefore, the left hand catches the scarf thrown by the right hand and the right

hand catches the scarf thrown by the left hand. (Two different colored scarves can be helpful in this activity.)

9. Juggling with three scarves
   o Give each student three scarves.
   o Students will start with two scarves in one hand and one scarf in the other.
   o The hand that is holding two scarves will throw one up in the air to the other side of the body.
   o The rest of the pattern is the same as with two scarves but the hands must move faster.
   o The motion is a constant crossing and throwing of the scarf in the right hand and the left hand with one scarf airborne at all times.

Figure 4.3   Juggling With Three Scarves

10. Juggling with balls or other objects
   o The directions are the same as for the juggling explained earlier, except students are given balls or objects to juggle.
   o This will be much more challenging for students.

o It may be beneficial to spend more time with one or two objects before allowing students to try three.

o You can also add challenges such as under the leg or arm, behind the back, and over the shoulder.

WHAT ARE 18 MOVEMENT ACTIVITIES THAT DEVELOP THE VESTIBULAR SYSTEM AND SPATIAL AWARENESS?

Spinning

1. One-legged hop and spin

   o Have students bend their knee so their right foot is close to their buttocks.

   o Now with their left hand, they will reach behind their back and grab their right foot.

   o While hopping on their left foot, they will spin in a clockwise rotation (then counterclockwise).

   o Have students bend their left knee so their left foot is close to their buttocks.

   o Have them reach their right hand behind their back and grab their left foot.

   o While hopping on their right foot, they will spin in a clockwise rotation (then counterclockwise).

2. Hand spin

   o Have students put their hands on the floor while their buttocks are held in the air. Students can have either their feet grounded or they can be up on their toes (head is pointing down).

Figure 4.4   Hand Spin

o Have students move their feet around their hands in a clockwise rotation (then counterclockwise).

o Be sure the hands stay in the same general area while the feet move around the hands in a circular pattern.

3. Crab walk spin

o Have students sit on their buttocks on the floor with their knees bent so their feet are flat. Hands are placed on the floor behind their back with their fingers pointing away from their body.

o Now, have students lift their buttocks off the ground so their feet and arms/hands are holding their weight.

o While keeping their hands in the same area, their feet will rotate in a circular, clockwise position around the hands (then counterclockwise).

4. Jumping jack spin

o Have students start by standing tall with their feet together and their arms down at their sides.

o Have students jump and separate their feet to slightly shoulder width apart while bringing their arms together up in the air.

o Continue with pattern while spinning clockwise (then counterclockwise).

5. 360-degree spin

o Have students stand with their feet shoulder width apart and their arms reaching out to the sides.

o Using a swing-like motion with their arms, have students jump and spin their hips, legs, and feet in a clockwise rotation.

o The goal is to spin 360 degrees and land back in the original position.

o Students will complete three or four spins in this direction then try counterclockwise.

Balancing

6. Arabesque walking

o Have students stand on their right foot (straight leg).

o Students will lift their left leg backward as far as they can without bending it. This will result in the upper body becoming parallel with the floor.

o Arms should be reaching out on the sides of the body (like an airplane).

Figure 4.5   Arabesque Walking

- Students will now come back to the starting position while stepping forward with the left foot and performing the task again.
- Continue a few times as students walk forward four to five steps.

7. Tree pose

- Have students stand with feet shoulder width apart.
- Students will place most of their weight on their right leg.
- They will bend their left leg into the inner thigh of the right leg (ankle or below knee for students that are struggling).
- Students will place their palms together as they lift their arms high in the air.
- Allow students to switch legs and try the pose again.

Figure 4.6   Tree Pose

8. Side plank
   - ○ Have students get into a push-up position (arms and toes holding the body).
   - ○ Students will shift their weight to their right arm as they roll on to the side of their right foot.

Figure 4.7   Side Plank

○ Both legs will be straight as the left foot and leg is stacked on top of the right.
○ The left arm will point to the ceiling.
○ Have students roll back to the center and do the other side.

9. Chair balance
○ Have students sit at the edge of their chairs.
○ Students will wrap their hands around the seat of the chair.
○ Allow students to lift their body off the chair while slightly lowering their body to the floor directly in front of the chair.
○ Ask students to straighten their legs while lifting one in the air.
○ Have them hold this position and then switch legs.

Figure 4.8   Chair Balance

Jumping

10. Leap frog
○ Have students get in a squatted position on the floor with their knees bent and their hands on the floor in front of them.
○ On command, students will push from their legs to leap in the air and land just in front of their original position.
○ Students can also do lateral leaps by jumping to the right or left of their original position.
○ This requires some space depending on how many leaps students take.
○ In tight spaces, have students leap in the air and come straight down as opposed to leaping forward.

11. Pattern jumping and hopping

   o Make hopscotch patterns around the room (use spots, Hula Hoops, paper plates, tape on the floor, etc.).
   o Place students in small groups of five or six.
   o Have students hop on one foot to the first, single spot.
   o Next, students will jump to the two following spots.
   o The pattern will be hop, jump, hop, jump, and so on.

12. Chair jumping

   o Have students get a partner.
   o Assign one student to be the jumper and one to be the spotter.
   o The jumper will stand on their chair or something of similar height in the room. (Please note that some chairs may not be conducive to this activity).
   o The spotter will balance the chair to make sure that it does not move during the jump.
   o When the spotter says, "Jump," and the person on the chair will jump to the ground and land on two feet.
   o The spotter can help balance the jumper once he or she contacts the floor if needed.
   o Have the partners switch roles.
   o Allow each person three or four turns at jumping off the chair.

13. Across the line

   o Students can do this activity by themselves, with a partner, or in a small group.
   o Find or make lines on the floor with tape.
   o Have students jump across the line.
   o Students will then take one step farther from the line and try again.
   o Students will continue to back away from the line until they can no longer make the jump.
   o Objects such as books, balls, clothing, and the like can also be used for this activity.

Combinations

14. Ball pass combination

   o Allow students to find a partner.
   o Give each pair a ball, and have them practice throwing the ball back and forth (Round 1).
   o After approximately 30 seconds, have students throw and catch the ball while jumping up and down (Round 2).
   o For Round 3, have students hop up and down on one leg while throwing and catching the ball.

○ For the final round, have students hop up and down on one leg and close one eye while throwing and catching the ball.

15. Arm circle hopping
   ○ Ask students to hop up and down on their right leg.
   ○ While hopping, have them make large arm circles with both arms circling forward (then circle arms backward).
   ○ Have students switch to their left leg and attempt the same task.

16. Jog plus wrist/elbow/shoulder tap
   ○ While jogging in place, have students reach their arms out to their sides.
   ○ Students will take their right arm and reach it across their body to touch their wrist, elbow, and shoulder on the left arm (make sure the left arm remains straight out to the side).
   ○ Then, while students continue to jog, have them reach their left arm across their body to touch their wrist, elbow, and shoulder on their right arm (keep the right arm straight out to the side of the body).
   ○ Continue this pattern.

17. Scissors kick plus arm cross
   ○ Have students begin by placing their arms high in the air and staggering their feet one in front of the other.
   ○ Students will jump and switch the position of their feet while crossing their arms in the air at the same time (right arm in front of left).
   ○ Then have students switch the position of their feet once again while their arms cross the other way (left arm in front of right).
   ○ Allow students to choose their speed.

18. Jumping up and down plus clapping game
   ○ Students will jump and down on two feet while playing some type of clapping game.
   ○ Clapping game suggestions are patty-cake, Miss-Mary-Mack, and handshake creations (or school appropriate games that students already know).

These 18 activities can serve as a starting point. Many movement exercises can be used or created where students cross the midline of their body. When planning activities that include spinning, balancing, and/or jumping, think back to when you were a child. The goal of these activities is to improve brain function and communication. When you see the results you desire, you will be inspired to continue to incorporate brain-compatible movements that prepare the brain for learning.

Chapter 4 Recap

- Consider your lesson goals when deciding which brain-compatible movements to use and when to use them.

- When asking students to read or write, consider having them participate in movements that cross the midline of the body or activities that develop the vestibular system.

- Look for windows that present an ideal opportunity to prepare the brain for learning.

- Be creative in your thinking as you design ideas for students to anchor the content while performing brain-compatible movements.

- Please keep in mind the philosophy presented in this book supports the notion that if these specific movements do not stimulate the brain as intended, they serve as effective brain breaks and activities that support exercise and fitness. Therefore, the activities presented in this chapter present a win-win approach.

- This chapter provides 10 movement activities that cross the midline of the body and can be used to improve visual tracking: (1) grapevine; (2) heel taps; (3) windmills; (4) hand clapping—toe tapping; (5) head–shoulders–knees–toes; (6) body taps; and progressive juggling with (7) one, (8) two, and (9) three scarves or (10) other objects.

- This chapter provides 18 movement activities that can be used to develop the vestibular system and spatial awareness: (1) one-legged hop and spin, (2) hand spin, (3) crab walk spin, (4) jumping jack spin, (5) 360-degree spin, (6) arabesque walking, (7) tree pose, (8) side plank, (9) chair balance, (10) leap frog, (11) pattern jumping and hoping, (12) chair jumping, (13) across the line, (14) ball pass combination, (15) arm circle hoping, (16) jog plus wrist/elbow/shoulder tap, (17) scissors kick plus arm cross, and (18) jumping up and down plus clapping game.

5

Providing Brain Breaks

> ⇨ Do all brain breaks have the same goal?
>
> ⇨ What are 22 brain breaks that can be done in two minutes or less?
>
> ⇨ Can these activities be modified to fit the grade level and physical capability of my students?

DO ALL BRAIN BREAKS HAVE THE SAME GOAL?

The previously stated objective of a brain break is to give the brain time away from the academic content. This is the primary goal of all brain breaks. It is important to note that brain breaks often have secondary goals that may differ slightly from one another. Numerous brain breaks are presented to explore with your students. Many brain breaks are simply meant to be fun and silly. Laughter is not only healthy for students, but also it is a great motivator (Shade, 1996). Some of the brain breaks will require some physical skill on behalf of the student. Other brain breaks will engage the brain in higher-level thinking and problem solving. Remember that as students participate in these activities, they are giving their hippocampus (the part of the brain that is responsible for the conversion of working memory to long-term memory) a much needed break. This is the most important purpose of brain breaks.

It is imperative to consider when and how to integrate brain breaks into lesson plans. Some brain breaks might be easier to implement than others. This is a personal issue, and it should be considered carefully. Start with the activities that best fit you and your students. Some of the suggested brain breaks might encourage silliness, but often, humor is a secondary goal. If you are concerned that students might be unwilling to try the activities, refer to Chapter 3 (Classroom Management) and be prepared to respond quickly and appropriately to these students.

The brain breaks that are recommended in this book will take approximately two minutes. This time can be slightly extended when students are engaged in the activities for the first time. As students become familiar with these activities, begin to refer to them by name. A poster listing the brain breaks would be a great addition to the classroom. These activities can help introduce movement in your classroom. Allow your creative thoughts to flow as you ultimately begin to add to the list.

WHAT ARE 22 BRAIN BREAKS THAT TAKE TWO MINUTES OR LESS?

1. Rock–paper–scissors snatch
   - Students will be placed in pairs while facing each other.
   - Both students say the catchphrase "rock–paper–scissors snatch" at the same time.
   - A student can show rock (a closed fist), paper (a flat hand, palm facing down), or scissors (index and middle finger spread apart, other fingers closed into the palm) after the catchphrase is spoken.
   - The following rules will be used to determine a winner: Paper beats rock because it covers it; scissors beats paper because it cuts it; rock beats scissors because it breaks it.
   - The winner of the bout can earn a point if he quickly snatches the hand of his opponent.
   - The loser of the bout attempts to withdraw her hand before it is snatched.
   - If the player who loses the bout snatches the other player's hand instead of pulling her hand away, the result is an immediate point for the other player.
   - This game can also be played successfully without points.

2. Three shakes
   - Instruct students to stand up, move around the room, and create three distinctive (school appropriate) handshakes with three different people.
   - Encourage students to use their hands, elbows, knees, and feet.

3. Body writing
   - Have students stand up and get into their personal space.
   - Instruct students to do the following:
     a. Write their last name in the air with the top of their head.
     b. Write their favorite animal in the air with their right elbow.
     c. Write their best friend's name in the air with their left elbow.
     d. Write what they had for breakfast with their right hip.
     e. Finally, if they could have any dessert they wanted, what would it be? Write it with your left hip.
     f. The educator can change these questions to fit their students' interests.

4. Hot potato or imaginary hot potato
   - Ask all students to stand up.
   - This game can be played in a circle or a random formation.
   - The directions for hot potato are as follows.
     a. The teacher will play some music as students pass a ball around the room.
     b. Players should pass the ball quickly so they aren't caught with it when the music stops.
     c. A second goal is to *not* have the ball in your hands when the music stops (or be the last one to have thrown it).
     d. This game can be played as an elimination activity, but it does not need to be.
   - The directions for imaginary hot potato are as follows.
     a. One student starts by throwing an imaginary object to someone else in the room.
     b. The thrower must act as if they are throwing the object they have announced.
     c. The receiver must catch it as if it were that object (e.g., a dirty diaper, a football, an Italian sandwich).
     d. After the object is thrown to a student, he or she sits down.
     e. Once everyone is sitting down, another round can be played or the teacher can move on to something new.

5. Triangle tag
   - Divide your class into groups of four. (This also works well with three.)
   - Three players form a triangle by holding hands; one of them is selected to be "It."
   - The fourth player stands outside the group and tries to tag whoever is It.
   - The triangle team spins to protect the It player from being tagged!

- The outside player and the It player switch places once the It player is tagged, and the role is then rotated. (A switch can also occur after a certain amount of time has passed.)
- Please note that although this game can be played in a classroom at a slower speed, it will be more effective in a larger space. (This is a great opportunity to take your students outside!)

6. Tag: everyone's "It"
   - Have all your students' stand up and space themselves around the room.
   - Everyone is It for a game of tag. (Walking only in a classroom setting or jogging in a larger space.)
   - Students move around the room trying to tag as many people as they can while trying to avoid being tagged.
   - Last one not touched is the winner.

7. Finger snatch
   - Have students stand facing a partner.
   - Each student puts their right hand out in front of them, palm facing up, and puts their left pointer finger in the palm of their opponent.
   - When the teacher says go, students, simultaneously, try to grab the other person's pointer finger and pull their pointer finger out of the palm of the other person.

8. Cement feet
   - Have students stand facing a partner approximately an arm length away.
   - Instruct students to put both of their hands directly out in front of them (palms facing their partner).
   - Partners will try to knock each other off balance by tapping hands or moving hands away when their opponent comes at them.
   - The student who knocks their partner's feet out of the cement wins that particular round.
   - Students lose if they touch any part of their partner's body except their hands.

9. Freeze dance
   - Allow students to stand up and find their personal space.
   - Play some fun, energetic music for the students to dance to.
   - When the teacher turns the music off, students have to try to freeze in the last position they were in exactly when the music stopped. (Hold that position!)

10. Busy city
    - This game is meant to represent a city during rush hour.
    - Students will move all around the room when the teacher begins the activity.

- o Students can choose their direction and their speed.
- o The most important rule is that they do this without touching any other student.
- o Encourage students to use manners, such as "excuse me," and "pardon me," as they walk near one another's personal space.
- o In time, the teacher may also want to allow students to perform other locomotor skills, such as galloping, skipping, or sliding.

11. Back-to-back passing

- o Place students in pairs or ask them to find a partner.
- o Explain to your students that they will stand back-to-back with their partner.
- o Give each team something to pass (e.g., ball, beanbag, marble).
- o When the music goes on, students will twist their shoulders and hips to the right as they pass the object to their partner.
- o They will then twist to their left to receive the object from their partner.
- o Encourage partners to pass the object as fast as they can without dropping it.
- o When the music stops, students will change directions.

12. Back-to-back stand up, sit down

- o Put students in pairs with someone who is close to their size. (This activity can still be very effective if sizes vary, although it will be more challenging.)
- o Ask students to sit on the floor, while leaning their backs against one another.
- o Knees should be bent while feet are placed flat on the floor.
- o The goal for students is to apply an equal amount of force against each other's back as they slowly begin to rise to their feet simultaneously.
- o Have students interlock elbows to discourage the use of their hands.

13. Social walk and talk

- o Ask students to find a partner.
- o Encourage students to choose someone new as a partner (refrain from choosing a friend so they can develop important social skills).
- o Allow students to take a social walk around the room.
- o The goal is just for students to talk as they circulate around the room.
- o The teacher may want to assign a topic (e.g., hobbies, favorite type of music, or favorite place to visit).
- o It is also appropriate to allow students to choose their topic while allowing the conversation to take a natural direction.

14. Hacky sack

   o Give students one to two minutes to see how many times a small group or even partners can continuously tap a hacky sack back and forth before it hits the ground.
   o Remind students that feet, knees, legs, chest, and head can be used.
   o The teacher may want to eliminate the use of the head if they see a potential concern. Make a hacky sack by balling up paper and wrapping it generously with tape.

15. Beanbag/Koosh ball toss

   o Assign or allow students to choose a partner.
   o Give students a beanbag, Koosh ball, or another type of ball.
   o Students will toss the object back and forth for the allotted time.
   o Music also accompanies this activity well.

16. Snatch it

   o Students can play this game by sitting at a desk or getting down on the floor on their hands and knees.
   o The teacher will give each team, which will be made up of two players, an object (e.g., a ball, beanbag, or an eraser) to place in the center of them.
   o The students must place their hands an equal distance away from the ball or object.
   o The teacher will then say one of two commands: right or left.
   o If the teacher says right, the students must react quickly to try to snatch the ball with their right hand.
   o If the teacher says left, the students must react quickly to try to snatch the ball with their left hand.
   o The goal is for students to try to snatch the ball before their partner does.

17. Taps

   o The teacher will allow students to get a partner (Student 1, Student 2).
   o Students will face each other with approximately an arm length distance between them.
   o Student 1 will reach out both hands (palms up).
   o Student 2 will place both her hands on top of her partner's palms.
   o Student 1 is in control of the game.
   o By using his right or left hand, Student 1 will quickly try to flip his hand to palm down while attempting to tap his partner's hand that is setting on top of his.
   o Student 2 who has her hands placed on the top must quickly pull her hand away before her opponent taps it.
   o After a few turns, instruct partners to reverse roles.

18. Back-to-back toss and catch

    o Ask students to stand back-to-back with a partner (Student 1, Student 2).
    o Give students an object to play with in the game (e.g., ball, beanbag, balloon, or beach ball).
    o As students stand back-to-back, Student 1 will throw the ball gently in the air behind her head.
    o Student 2 must react quickly to try to catch the object.
    o Students will take turns throwing and catching while remaining back-to-back.

19. Elbow trick

    o Instruct students to stand up and find their personal space.
    o Give each student a beanbag.
    o Explain that students will bend their arm so their elbow is pointing out away from their body.
    o Have students place the beanbag on their elbow.
    o When they feel ready, they snap their hand down to try to catch the beanbag that is being thrown from the elbow.
    o If students experience success, the teacher can allow them to use more-challenging objects, such as an eraser or two beanbags.

20. Foot-to-foot passing

    o Ask students to get a partner (Student 1, Student 2).
    o Give each pair one beanbag.
    o Student 1 will place the beanbag on her foot.
    o She will then try to pass it to her partner's foot without using her hands.
    o Encourage students to see how many passes they can make before the beanbag hits the floor.

21. Drop–clap–catch

    o Have students find a partner (Student 1, Student 2).
    o Give each pair one ball.
    o Student 1 will stand with his back to Student 2.
    o Student 2 will place the ball against the neck of Student 1.
    o On the count of three, Student 2 will release her hands from the ball.
    o Student 1 will attempt to catch the ball behind his back.
    o If Student 1 does this successfully, he will advance to the second round.
    o The second round presents the same challenge except now Student 1 will try to clap his hands before he catches the ball behind his back.
    o The partners will then switch roles.

22. Throw–spin–catch

- o Ask all students to find a partner (Student 1, Student 2).
- o Give each pair a ball.
- o Student 1 will take her turn while Student 2 ensures a safe environment by making sure other groups keep their distance.
- o Student 1 will throw the ball in the air about three to four feet above her head.
- o When the ball is in the air, she will spin completely around one time and try to catch the ball before it hits the floor.
- o The partners will then switch roles.

CAN THESE ACTIVITIES BE MODIFIED TO FIT THE GRADE LEVEL AND PHYSICAL CAPABILITY OF MY STUDENTS?

When reading about or learning any new activity, it is imperative to consider the following student characteristics:

- Age
- Physical skill
- Maturity level
- Cognitive ability

Many activities can be altered to fit students with many different needs and ability levels. Sometimes changes can be small, such as using a larger or smaller ball in the activity. Other adjustments may take more consideration to change rules and directions while maintaining a similar goal. For example, a kindergarten teacher might find that rock–paper–scissors snatch is too difficult for this particular age group. These students could just learn the game of rock–paper–scissors first. The part of the game where students try to snatch their opponent's hand could be a rule that is added to the game later in the year.

If your intention is to simplify an activity, you must first reflect on what aspect might make it difficult for your students. Are there too many rules? Are the rules too complex? Are your students lacking the coordination to perform the challenge at hand? There are a number of ways to make an activity easier for younger students or individuals with special needs. Here are some suggestions:

- Use a larger ball or object.
- Use a softer ball or object.
- Choose a ball or object that will not drop to the floor as quickly (such as a beach ball).
- Have students stand closer together.

- Chunk the game into smaller sections.
- Encourage students to take their time (slow things down).
- Demonstrate the activity with more than one group.

When working with older students or individuals who have a higher skill level, it is essential that changes be made to activities to meet these students' needs. To make an activity more challenging, a close examination of the rules and directions is required. Here are some suggestions for making an activity more difficult:

- Use a smaller ball or object.
- Choose a ball or object that is more dense and will fall quicker.
- Increase the number of times a task or trick must be completed.
- Complicate the rules.
- Increase or decrease the number of people involved in the task (depends on the brain break).
- Set time limits.

Not all students will take pleasure in every activity in which they participate. Personality types, likes, and dislikes will play a role in a student's enjoyment of an activity. Therefore, it is important to vary the brain breaks previously listed. It is human nature to do what makes us comfortable. Many teachers will find specific brain breaks to their liking and will be tempted to use the same ones repeatedly. Branching out and trying new things will keep your students guessing.

Chapter 5 Recap

- The primary goal of all brain breaks is to give the brain time away from the academic content.

- Brain breaks have secondary goals such as humor, problem solving, and higher-level thinking.

- The most important purpose of brain break is to give the hippocampus (the part of the brain that is responsible for the conversion of working memory to long-term memory) the opportunity to process and consolidate the content that was previously taught.

- Start by choosing the brain breaks for your students that you feel the most comfortable with.

- Refer to Chapter 3 (Classroom Management) when you feel concerned about student behavior.

(Continued)

(Continued)

- Consider making a poster for your classroom that lists the brain breaks. When you feel ready, add your ideas to the list.

- There are 22 brain breaks contained in this chapter that the educator can implement into his or her lessons in two minutes or less: (1) rock–paper–scissors snatch, (2) three shakes, (3) body writing, (4) hot potato or imaginary hot potato, (5) triangle tag, (6) tag: everyone's "It," (7) finger snatch, (8) cement feet, (9) freeze dance, (10) busy city, (11) back-to-back passing, (12) back-to-back stand up, sit down, (13) social walk and talk, (14) hacky sack, (15) beanbag/Koosh ball toss, (16) snatch it, (17) taps, (18) back-to-back toss and catch, (19) elbow trick, (20) foot-to-foot passing, (21) drop–clap–catch, and (22) throw–spin–catch.

- When reading about or learning any new activity, it is imperative that the educator consider the following characteristics about their students: age, physical skill, maturity level, and cognitive ability.

- Simplify activities by using a larger ball or object, choosing a ball or object that will not drop to the floor as quickly, allowing students to stand closer together, chunking games into smaller sections, encouraging students to take their time, and demonstrating the activity with more than one group.

- Make activities more challenging by using a smaller ball or object, choosing a ball or object that is more dense and will fall quicker, increasing the number of times a task or trick must be completed, complicating the rules, increasing or decreasing the number of people involved in the task (depends on the brain break), and setting time limits.

- Refrain from using the same brain breaks repeatedly. Keep your students guessing.

6

Supporting Exercise and Fitness

> ⇨ How can exercise and fitness be supported in the classroom? What if I am not currently active in my life?
>
> ⇨ What are some basic elements of movement that can be used effectively in a classroom environment?
>
> ⇨ What are various exercises for the classroom that can be implemented in one to five minutes?
>
> ⇨ What can I do to help make fitness fun?

HOW CAN EXERCISE AND FITNESS BE SUPPORTED IN THE CLASSROOM? WHAT IF I AM NOT CURRENTLY ACTIVE IN MY LIFE?

The choice to be physically fit is yours alone. Many Americans lead an inactive lifestyle. Maintaining a high level of fitness takes a great deal of time and effort. Exercise is hard work and is often perceived as boring. These feelings are normal. There are many reasons for making exercise and fitness a part of your everyday routine; the most important is your health and well-being. Human nature desires a healthy mind, body, and soul. However, teachers have a serious time commitment to their profession. For many, the result is no time available for exercising. Or is there?

If you are not physically active, implementing exercise and fitness in your classroom is a perfect opportunity to make life changes. Have you considered exercising with your students? This would be an achievable place to begin. This fitness commitment can be made by simply engaging with your students in physical activities for one minute every school day. Everyone has one minute to give to exercise! This minute can be built into your classroom schedule. You might then consider extending this exercise regimen to your personal life. There are many fitness activities provided in this chapter, each taking only one to five minutes. It's a great opportunity to make changes for yourself and your students.

If you're saying to yourself, "But I hate exercise!" remember this feeling is common and acceptable. Think about all the responsibilities you endure. Do you enjoy all of them? Of course not! By supporting exercise and fitness in your classroom, you are providing yourself with time to exercise. Therefore, lack of time can no longer be your excuse. Now, all you need is the motivation! Allow your students to motivate you. More than likely, you have students who feel the same way about exercise. Explain to your students that the goal is to develop healthy habits about exercise and fitness. In turn, you become an important role model.

Supporting exercise and fitness in your classroom does have a distinct purpose. This opportunity is not just opening the door for you to incorporate exercise in your life; it is also providing a brain break for students. Also, as explained in Chapter 1, physically fit children are performing better academically. Exercise increases oxygen and blood to the brain. This wakes up both the body and brain and enhances the learning process. The important message about fitness will be clearly heard when all teachers in a school building support exercise and fitness in the classroom as well as in the gymnasium.

If you have physical or personal reasons why you are not exercising, you can still support it in the classroom. There is a very simple way to proceed, and this chapter will offer plenty of basic fitness suggestions. Hanging a poster in your room describing and showing the exercises would be beneficial. It is realistic to assume that you have at least one student in your classroom who is familiar with the exercises and would be willing to demonstrate them for the class.

Students might truly enjoy being asked to come to the front of the room, choose an exercise from the poster and lead their classmates through it for one minute. Many students will be motivated by this opportunity simply to get out of their seat. Students who are not motivated would be more comfortable following the leader. Either way, students are moving, exercising, and building healthy habits.

WHAT ARE SOME BASIC ELEMENTS OF MOVEMENT THAT CAN BE USED EFFECTIVELY IN A CLASSROOM ENVIRONMENT?

There are many different ways to move a body. Unfortunately, people of all fitness levels continually tend to repeat the same or similar activities. Take, for instance, an avid runner. Can an individual who chooses running as their only source of exercise still improve their fitness level? Absolutely! However, what might happen if the runner abruptly changes her workout and participates in a kickboxing class? Chances are she will be sore the next day because her body is not use to kickboxing. What does this have to do with movement in the classroom?

It is healthy to move the body in many different ways through various activities and exercises. As you begin to support exercise and fitness, variety will offer novelty. Remember, the brain seeks novelty. There are three distinct categories of movement: (1) locomotor, (2) nonlocomotor, and (3) manipulative skills. As you view nontraditional ways to encourage students to move, ask the question, how and when can I use this during my lessons?

Locomotor movements refer to traveling skills that allow a person to go from one point to another. The most common locomotor movements are walking and jogging. Although walking is very suitable for a classroom environment, there are five suggested movements to consider. These five locomotor skills are as follows:

1. Skip

2. Slide

3. Gallop

4. Hop

5. Leap

Imagine asking your students to skip or gallop to the whiteboard to solve a math problem. This would be an easy request on your part, and many students would love it! If you have ever seen a group of people skipping (any age), you may also have noticed them smiling. It is hard to frown when you are skipping and galloping. These locomotor movements tend to bring pleasure. Consider some of the brain breaks or class cohesion activities discussed earlier. Choosing a locomotor skill other than walking may make the activity more enjoyable. Be sure to consider your space and the typical speed of the movement.

Nonlocomotor skills are performed in place. Many activities help develop these skills.

Here are five examples of nonlocomotor movements that would work effectively in a classroom:

1. Shake

2. Twist

3. Stretch

4. Bend

5. Swing

If you are searching for a new brain break, put on some music and teach your students the twist, or allow them to get up and stretch if they have been sitting for longer than 15 to 20 minutes. These nonlocomotor movements are quick and fun to implement. Many of your creative students will enjoy the numerous activities you can generate with nonlocomotor actions.

Manipulative movements include activities that develop gross motor skills. Gross motor skills involve large muscle groups or movement of the whole body. Activities that build manipulative skills are engaging for many students. Kinesthetic learners typically love to use their body to learn a skill or perform a physical task. Many different movements can be used to improve gross motor skills. Here are a few examples appropriate for the classroom:

- Throw/catch
- Bounce/dribble
- Volley
- Balance
- Push-pull

This book provides many activities to develop manipulative skills. Other forms of movement that benefit gross motor development can be designed. For example, allowing students to continually throw and catch a ball while practicing their multiplication facts is a notable case in point. An activity such as this can be very motivating. This can be used advantageously while initiating this purpose of movement.

WHAT ARE VARIOUS EXERCISES FOR THE CLASSROOM THAT CAN BE IMPLEMENTED IN ONE TO FIVE MINUTES?

To gain a better understanding of how to engage students in exercise, it is beneficial to be familiar with the health-related components of fitness. These components are designed to promote healthy living. The four components addressed in this book are the following:

1. Cardio-respiratory endurance

2. Muscular strength

3. Muscular endurance

4. Flexibility

Knowing these components will help you deliver well-rounded work-outs as you vary the exercises. Even if you have students engage in a physical exercise once a week for one minute, each week should present a different activity that provides a new challenge. For example, if you asked students to stand up and complete 25 jumping jacks one week, you might try push-ups the following week.

Cardio-respiratory endurance allows the heart, lungs, and blood vessels to work together while performing whole-body activities. Here are 15 classroom exercises to promote cardio-respiratory endurance.

1. Jumping jacks

   ○ Have students stand tall with their feet together and their arms down at their sides.
   ○ Have students jump separating their feet to shoulder width apart while bringing their arms together in the air.
   ○ Continue with the pattern.

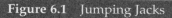

Figure 6.1   Jumping Jacks

2. Scissors kicks
   ○ Have students begin by placing their arms on their hips and staggering feet one in front of the other.
   ○ Jump and switch the position of their feet.

3. Cross lateral hops
   ○ Have students bring their right elbow to their left knee while hopping one time on their right foot.
   ○ Then bring left elbow to right knee while hopping on left foot.
   ○ Continue the pattern.

Figure 6.2   Cross Lateral Hops

4. Jog in place
   ○ Have students pick their feet up and down while staying in one place.

5. Line jumps
   - Have students find a line on the floor.
   - While keeping their feet together and continuing to face the same direction, jump to the other side.
   - Continue jumping back and forth across the line.

6. Crisscrosses
   - Have students stand with their feet slightly more than shoulder width apart.
   - Jump while overlapping their feet (right foot in front, left foot behind).
   - Jump back to feet being slightly more than shoulder width apart.
   - Jump together, switching the foot that is in the front (left foot in front, right foot behind).
   - Continue the pattern.

Figure 6.3   Crisscrosses

7. Box jumps
   - Have students imagine a box or square on the floor with four separate quadrants.
   - While keeping their feet close together, jump into one quadrant.
   - Continue by making a circular or crisscross pattern while jumping into each quadrant.

8. Mountain climbers
   - Have students place their hands on the floor directly underneath their shoulders.
   - Then, stagger feet so that one foot is placed on the floor beneath the chest with a bent knee, and the other leg is straightened (get on toes).
   - Jump and switch the position of their feet.
   - Continue to switch feet.

Figure 6.4   Mountain Climbers

9. Jump twists
   - Have students stand with their hips facing forward.
   - Next, they jump and twist their hips to the right.
   - Jump and go back to the forward position.
   - Jump and twist hips to the left.
   - Follow the pattern forward, right, forward, left.

10. High knees
    - Have students walk in place bringing their knees high toward their chest with each step.

11. Glute kicks
    - ○ Have students walk in place bringing the heels of their feet back to their buttocks with each step.

12. Jump tucks
    - ○ Have students jump in the air bringing their knees to their chest.
    - ○ Bring knees as high as possible.

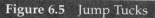

Figure 6.5 Jump Tucks

13. Squat jumps
    - ○ Have students bend down and touch their hands to the floor while keeping their back straight, head up, and feet shoulder width apart.
    - ○ Next, they jump high in to the air (raise hands to the ceiling).

Figure 6.6   Squat Jumps

14. Head, shoulders, knees, and toes
    o Have students touch their head, then their shoulders, knees, and toes.
    o Increase speed to build the challenge.

15. Jump rope
    o Have students jump to clear an imaginary rope.
    o They should swing their arms around their body while coordinating the jumps.

Basic Tips for Unfit Students

1. Start slow

2. Do not lift knees or feet high in the air

3. Keep a steady pace

4. Pause in the middle of certain movements

5. When jumping, stay low to the ground (refrain from jumping if it is too difficult)

Basic Tips for Fit Students

1. Keep a faster, consistent pace

2. Lift feet and knees high in the air

3. Refrain from pausing during the exercise

4. Jump as high as they can

5. Choose to slow down when they are tired as opposed to pausing

Muscular strength is the amount of force that your muscles can exert at any given time. Muscular endurance is the ability of the same muscles to work for an extended period before failing. These components will be united in this book to provide simple exercises that encourage overall muscular growth. The muscular activities are broken down into three sections: arms, legs, and core. Choose exercises from all three areas to develop muscles throughout the body.

Arms

1. Arm curl
   - Have students stand with their arms at their sides.
   - Squeeze fists together.
   - Bend elbows to bring both of their arms to their shoulders.
   - Tighten the muscle in the upper arms and hold it for three seconds.

2. Tricep extension
   - Have students reach both arms in the air.
   - Then, make a fist with one hand and cover it with the other hand (keep arms close to their head).
   - Bend elbows while making sure they point straight out in front (continue to keep your arms close to their head).
   - Squeeze the back, upper part of the arm, and hold it for three seconds.
   - Continue to tighten the muscle throughout the movement.
   - Return to the beginning position where arms are straight in the air.

Figure 6.7   Tricep Extension

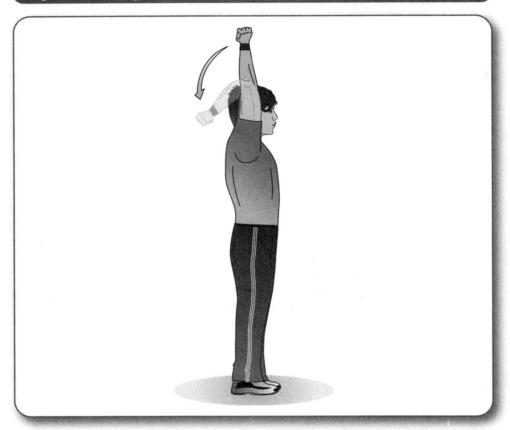

3. Front raise

   o Have students make two fists and lift their arms directly out in front of them.
   o Then, tighten their muscles in their shoulder and their arms.

4. Lateral raise

   o Have students make two fists and lift their arms out to their sides.
   o Then, tighten the muscles in their shoulders and their arms.

5. Chair dips

   o Have students sit on the edge of a chair.
   o Next, have them wrap their hands around the chair.
   o Then they lift their body off the chair and lower their body to the floor directly in front of the chair.
   o Keep knees bent and feet flat on the floor (straighten legs to present a greater challenge).
   o When the upper arm becomes parallel to the floor, straighten their arms so that they are holding their body above the seat of the chair.
   o Do not allow the buttocks to touch the chair.

Figure 6.8   Chair Dips

Legs

1. Squats

   - Have students stand with their feet shoulder width apart (or a bit wider).
   - Keep backs straight and look upward slightly.
   - Bend knees to lower buttocks closer to the floor.
   - When the top of the legs are parallel to the ground, stand up.
   - Do not bend too low on this exercise.
   - Only bend down until the top leg is parallel with the ground; choose a distance that feels comfortable.

Figure 6.9   Squats

2. Lunges

   - Have students stand in a wide, staggered stance with hips turned toward the front leg.

- ○ Bend front knee so that it is directly above the foot (do not allow the knee to pass by the foot).
- ○ Keep back leg fairly straight.
- ○ Begin to slightly bend the back knee as it moves closer to the ground.
- ○ Just before their knee touches the ground, slowly head back to the standing stance.
- ○ Remember to do the same number of repetitions on each leg.

Figure 6.10 Lunges

3. Wall seat

- ○ Find a wall.
- ○ Have students place their back against the wall and bend their knees until their upper leg is parallel with the floor.
- ○ Keep feet planted flat on the ground.
- ○ Hold this position for a designated time.

4. Calf raises

- ○ Have students stand with feet shoulder width apart.
- ○ Go up on their toes and squeeze the muscle in the back of the lower leg.

○ Hold this position for three seconds.

○ Point toes out or in to alter the challenge.

5. Leg extension

○ Have students sit in a chair.

○ They wrap their hands around the side of the chair.

○ Lift both legs directly out in front of them.

○ Tighten the muscles in upper leg and hold for three seconds.

○ Slowly return feet back to the floor.

Core

1. Push-ups

○ Have students place their hands on the floor, slightly more than shoulder width apart.

○ Straighten body like a board so as to balance on the hands and toes.

○ Bend elbows to lower body to the ground.

○ Go down toward the floor and then push back up.

○ To make this activity easier, place knees on the ground (remember to keep the body straight like a board).

○ Wall push-ups are also an easier alternative (same rules apply just push off the wall instead of the floor).

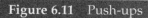

Figure 6.11   Push-ups

2. Crunches
   - Have students lie on the ground with their knees bent and feet placed flat on the ground.
   - Students cross their arms over their chest so their hands are near each shoulder.
   - Tighten abdominal muscles as the shoulder blades are lifted off the ground.
   - Hold the position for three seconds.
   - Slowly lower body back to the floor.

3. Elbow bridge (plank)
   - Have students straighten their body on the floor, facing down.
   - Using their forearms and toes, they lift their body off the floor.
   - Stay in position for the designated time.
   - Tighten muscles to hold pose.

Figure 6.12   Elbow Bridge

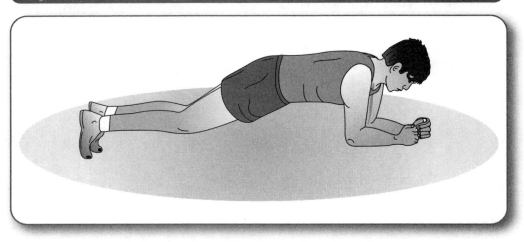

4. Superman
   - Have students straighten their body on the floor, facing down.
   - Place arms directly out in front them.
   - At the same time, lift both arms and legs off the ground and into the air.
   - Remember to keep legs straight.
   - Tighten the back and hold this position for three seconds.

Figure 6.13 Superman

5. V-seat

  ○ Have students sit on the floor.
  ○ They raise their arms and legs in the air at the same time, as to make the letter *V*.
  ○ Hold this position as long as possible.

Figure 6.14 V-Seat

Flexibility is the ability to move body parts and joints freely and easily through a wide range of motion. Here are a few areas of the body listed with accompanying stretches that can be performed in the classroom.

1. Sides of neck
   o Students sit or stand with arms hanging loosely at their sides.
   o Have them tilt their head sideways to the right and then to the left.
   o Hold for five seconds.

Figure 6.15 Sides of Neck

2. Shoulders, chest, and upper back
   o Have students interlace fingers behind their head.
   o Keep the upper body erect while pointing elbows out to the side.
   o Pull shoulder blades together.

Figure 6.16   Shoulders, Chest, and Upper Back

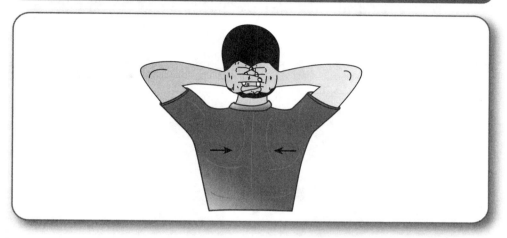

3. Shoulder and back of upper arms

   ○ Have students place their right hand over their left shoulder.
   ○ With left hand, pull right elbow across chest toward left shoulder and hold.
   ○ Repeat on other side.

Figure 6.17   Shoulders and Backs of Upper Arms

4. Shoulders and neck

- o Have students raise the top of their shoulders toward their ears.
- o Hold for five seconds, and then have them relax their shoulders.

Figure 6.18 Shoulders and Neck

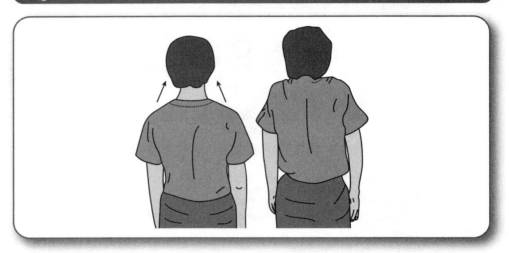

5. Chest, back, and shoulders

- o In one movement, have students lift their chest and raise their arms slightly below shoulder level.
- o Squeeze shoulder blades together with elbows bent.
- o Return to starting position.

Figure 6.19 Chest, Back, and Shoulders

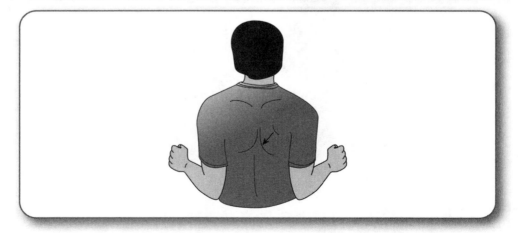

6. Hip and front of thigh

   ○ Have students stand with feet shoulder width apart.
   ○ Bring their heel slowly toward their buttocks until they feel the stretch.
   ○ Lower the leg back down.
   ○ Repeat with the other leg.

Figure 6.20 Hip and Front of Thigh

7. Front and back of thigh

   ○ Have students stand with their feet shoulder width apart.
   ○ Bring one knee slowly up toward their chest.
   ○ Then, lower their leg back down.
   ○ Repeat with the other leg.

Figure 6.21   Front and Back of Thigh

8. Inner thigh

   o Have students stand with feet slightly more than shoulder width apart.
   o Then, they bend their right hip slightly while moving their left hip downward toward the right knee.
   o Hold for five seconds.
   o Repeat on the other side.

9. Back of thigh and lower back

   o Have students lie down.
   o They then grab their upper leg just above and behind their knee.
   o Have them gently pull their bent leg toward their chest.
   o Repeat on the other side.

Figure 6.22   Inner Thigh

Figure 6.23   Back of Thigh and Lower Back

10. Back, side of hip, and neck

- ○ Have students sit on floor with their left leg straight out in front of them.
- ○ Bend right leg and place the right foot on the outside of the left leg.
- ○ Bend the left elbow and place it outside the right knee.
- ○ Place right hand behind hips on the floor.
- ○ Turn head over right shoulder while rotating the upper body to the right.
- ○ Hold for five seconds.
- ○ Repeat on the other side.

Figure 6.24   Back, Side of Hip, and Neck

What will determine how much time you spend supporting exercise and fitness in a classroom setting? Two significant factors come into play: your personality and your beliefs about the importance of exercise and fitness. If you are inactive, one minute might seem like more than enough time. However, if fitness plays a serious role in your life, you might consider consistently reinforcing its importance to your students. You may also be completely dissatisfied with the decline in the health and well-being of our young people. As a result, you may feel that supporting exercise and fitness in the classroom is an important step to addressing these concerns.

This book supports the idea of a one- to five-minute timeframe for exercise and fitness. If you have one minute to encourage exercise, you can choose one or two activities from the previous lists. If you have five minutes to give to this cause, you can choose one or two exercises from each of the five sections. Devote one complete minute to each of the following sections:

1. Cardio-respiratory endurance

2. Arms

3. Legs

4. Core

5. Flexibility

Recall the benefits of exercise and fitness that were discussed in Chapter 1. Remember that taking a few minutes away from academic content to incorporate this purpose of movement can actually improve learning efficiency. It is primarily the responsibility of the physical education teacher to implement exercise and fitness regimens in your school. However, a team approach between the physical education and classroom teachers would be valuable. State and national physical education standards have brought academics into the gymnasium so that curriculums may be crossed. It only seems appropriate to support exercise and fitness in the classroom.

WHAT CAN I DO TO HELP MAKE FITNESS FUN?

Many students will be motivated to engage in exercise and fitness activities while others will show some resistance as their lifestyles may consist of limited movement. Therefore, it is important to make fitness fun. Here are six strategies that can be used to increase the enjoyment of exercise and fitness.

1. Present a positive attitude
   o Being honest about the role that exercise plays in your life is an important factor.
   o Demonstrating excitement and passion whenever possible can inspire your students.
2. Add music
   o Adding upbeat music helps motivate students while making the workouts more enjoyable.
   o Allowing students to choose or supply their music whenever possible can be a great motivator.
3. Have students use partners
   o Encouraging students to work out with a partner will push them to try their best.
   o Permitting students to choose their partner often serves as a great motivator.

4. Present a challenge

   o Setting a goal for students to reach, such as, "How many mountain climbers can you do in one minute?" will add a spark to the workout.
   o Using time limits will create excitement for many students.

5. Focus on individual growth and improvement

   o Having students compete against themselves to beat their record takes the focus away from competition with others.
   o Encouraging students to support one another will provide a positive environment built on mutual respect.

6. Make it a game

   o Making the fitness workout a game will stimulate students to play. There are four sample games explained next that can help to make fitness fun: (1) fitness freeze, (2) balance challenge, (3) fitness tag, and (4) fitness musical chairs.

      o Fitness freeze: This game is the same as freeze dance (brain break) except students exercise when the music is on and freeze when it goes off.
      o Balance challenge: Have students participate in different balance poses (e.g., one leg, two body parts, three body parts, and the like). This is a great time to incorporate any yoga positions that you may know.
      o Fitness tag: This is a basic tag game. Choose anywhere from one to four people to be "It." Give the participants who are It something to show who they are (a ball or a scarf). Set a designated boundary area. This game is great outside if weather permits. Everyone will speed walk around the designated area while trying to avoid the people who are It. If someone is tagged by a person who is It, that individual is now frozen. Everyone can unfreeze themselves by performing an exercise for a certain number of times (e.g., 10 jumping jacks, 10 glute kicks, 10 squat jumps) Change players that are It every minute.
      o Fitness musical chairs: The arrangement of the room may vary depending on the number of participants and the size of the room. One interesting setup is to make two circles: one smaller circle in the center of the room and a larger circle around the outside of the smaller circle with chairs facing one another. This should make the game set-up look like a miniature track. You will have a few less chairs in the game than the number of participants who are playing. For example, if you have 30 people in a class and three people sitting at a table, then use 27 chairs in the game. The instructor will play some upbeat music as the participants move around the chairs/minitrack at a speed that is

safe and comfortable. When the music goes off, everyone finds a seat. The three people left standing will now be sitting at a given table at the conclusion of the game. Do not take any chairs out of the game. When the second round begins, the music is turned on and everyone begins to move around the chairs the other direction. Switching directions is important so that people do not get dizzy. This part of the rules is what makes this game unique. The three people who lost round one will now sit down on one of the chairs so that everyone will be moving around them. These participants will engage in a fitness workout/activity that the instructor will change for each round (e.g., bicep curl; shoulder raises; head, shoulder, knees, and toes; seated cross laterals; chair dips, and the like). After each round, three more people will join the fitness workout/activity.

Showing support for exercise, by implementing it in the classroom, takes very little time. Allowing students to engage in the 44 activities presented in this section along with the one- to five-minute approach is very possible. The knowledge required of the educator to accomplish this task is minimal and can be learned through the information contained herein. Developing an understanding of this information would allow the educator to move students in many different ways while exercising the entire body as it grows and matures.

Chapter 6 Recap

- Teachers can support exercise in their classroom by getting involved in the activities or choosing a student to be the leader.

- There are three basic elements of movement: (1) locomotor, (2) nonlocomotor, and (3) manipulative skills. It is beneficial to provide activities for students that incorporate all three elements of movement.

- Examples of locomotor movements are skipping, sliding, galloping, hopping, and leaping.

- Examples of nonlocomotor movements are shaking, twisting, stretching, bending, and swinging.

- Examples of manipulative skills are throwing/catching, bouncing/dribbling, volleying, balancing, pushing, and pulling.

- There are four health-related components of fitness discussed in this book: (1) cardio-respiratory endurance, (2) muscular strength, (3) muscular endurance, and (4) flexibility.

(Continued)

(Continued)

- There are 15 cardio-respiratory examples: (1) jumping jacks; (2) scissors kicks; (3) cross lateral hops; (4) jog in place; (5) line jumps; (6) criss-crosses; (7) box jumps; (8) mountain climbers; (9) jump twists; (10) high knees; (11) glute kicks; (12) jump tucks; (13) squat jumps; (14) head, shoulders, knees, and toes; and (15) jump rope.

- There are five muscular exercises for the arms: (1) arm curls, (2) tricep extensions, (3) front raises, (4) lateral raises, and (5) chair dips.

- There are five muscular exercises for the legs: (1) squats, (2) lunges, (3) wall seat, (4) calf raises, and (5) leg extensions.

- There are five muscular exercises for the core: (1) push-ups, (2) crunches, (3) elbow bridge/plank, (4) superman, and (5) V-seat.

- There are many different stretches for the neck, chest, back, arms, shoulders, and legs.

- There are six strategies to make fitness fun: (1) present a positive attitude, (2) add music, (3) have students partner up, (4) present a challenge, (5) focus on individual growth and improvement, and (6) make it a game.

- There are four fitness games to consider: (1) fitness freeze, (2) balance challenge, (3) fitness tag, and (4) fitness musical chairs.

7

Developing Class Cohesion

⇨ How often should class cohesion activities be used?

⇨ Is competition appropriate in class cohesion activities?

⇨ What are five class cohesion activities that build team unity?

⇨ What are nine class cohesion activities that encourage whole-group unity?

HOW OFTEN SHOULD CLASS COHESION ACTIVITIES BE USED?

Creating a comfortable, interconnected environment is beneficial to the learning process. However, these activities take time to implement in the classroom. Class cohesion activities are not intended for daily use. Therefore, the choice of when the most appropriate times throughout the year to engage students in these activities is critical. The beginning of the school year is an optimal time to incorporate class cohesion activities. This provides students with the opportunity to get to know one another's names, strengths, and personalities. Creating a friendly and comfortable classroom environment from the first day of school is important to the level of success experienced. Have you ever realized that halfway through the year some students do not even know one another's name? Who is at fault in this situation? Who is responsible for providing opportunities for students to call one another by name while participating in activities that require and build teamwork? Teachers can make this happen. Aside from the beginning of the school year, here are some suggested times to include students in class cohesion activities:

- Once a month for class periods that are 30 to 50 minutes
- Once every two weeks for class periods that are 90 minutes
- The day after a big test
- The day before or the day after a break in the school calendar
- When students are not connecting with one another

IS COMPETITION APPROPRIATE DURING CLASS COHESION ACTIVITIES?

Opinions differ about the role that competition serves concerning movement activities. Some individuals hold strong beliefs that competition is not necessary and should be avoided at all costs. The philosophy contained in this book will support the idea of a balance between competitive and noncompetitive activities. A heavier emphasis will be on activities that are noncompetitive to create an entire class working as one. However, allowing students to compete in certain situations is simply a part of life. Every student must learn the concept of winning graciously as well as losing respectfully. Children are often rewarded for participating in events or activities despite their success throughout the process. This is appropriate at times because effort is often a child's most important contribution. However, this may also raise some level of concern. Are children able to lose or fail at something while maintaining their composure? It appears that many children handle this sense of failure with anger, sadness, and disgust.

Philosophically speaking, this book will support two categories of class cohesion activities: (1) team unity and (2) whole-group unity. Many individuals are drawn to, or motivated by, competition. When implementing class cohesion activities, whether they're perceived as competitive, the most important aspect is presentation. Competition is meant to be positive. Learning how to cheer for and support teammates demonstrates kindness. Being confident to share a compliment with the opposing team shows pride and respect. Promoting an environment where everyone is a winner, even if the game is lost, teaches respect and sportsmanship. Many life lessons can be taught during competition.

Two examples of competition during class cohesion activities will be used. One is a team challenge and the other features the entire class competing against the clock. Class cohesion activities that build unity occur when teams challenge one another in select events. This form of competition builds togetherness, as teams must form strategies and demonstrate a joint effort to accomplish a task. The implementation of these activities will cause excitement among students. Promoting consideration toward teammates and opposing team members will be the focus for everyone. These activities are fun, energizing, and engaging for all students.

Class cohesion activities that build whole-group unity occur when the entire class is racing against the clock or engaging in a fun game together. These activities build an interconnected classroom environment. Students will need to support one another, follow the rules, and actively participate for the game and/or activity to succeed. Students will love to compete against the clock while racing to win the record of the day. Placing winning times on the board and comparing class-to-class scores may even excite students who are typically unmotivated during movement activities.

WHAT ARE FIVE CLASS COHESION ACTIVITIES THAT BUILD TEAM UNITY?

1. Balloon tap
   - Split the class into three or four equal teams (five to eight students in a group).
   - All team members will make a small, tight circle.
   - Members of each team must stay hooked together by either joining hands or linking forearms.
   - Each team is given a balloon that is close to the size of a volleyball (a beach ball can be used if there is a latex concern).
   - Each team has to stay linked together while tapping their balloon into the air.
   - The participants can use any part of their body to keep the balloon up; however, they need to play safely and be aware of other teammates.
   - After each team is given a few minutes to practice with one balloon, another balloon can be added.
   - If a balloon starts to drift away from a team, the entire team must stay linked together as they all move to get the balloon and keep it from hitting the ground.
   - After a few minutes of practice, the real game begins. This game is a friendly competition where one team is playing against the others.
   - The first team to earn three or five (teacher's decisions) points will be the winning team.
   - A team can earn a point by keeping its balloons in the air longer than the other teams.
   - As soon as a balloon hits the ground, the other teams earn a point.
   - Teams can be combined to increase the challenge.

o The goal is for both linked teams to keep all the balloons up in the air. (This is easier said than done.)

o Encourage participants to develop strategies.

o Set goals and see how many balloons students can keep up in the air at one time.

o Good luck trying to stop some of your participants from laughing!

2. Balloon volleyball

o Split the classroom into four quadrants that will make up four volleyball courts. (Desks work great for separating the courts.)

o Divide the class into eight equal teams.

o Two teams will play against each other on Court 1, two teams on Court 2, two teams on Court 3, and so on.

o In the center of each court, place two pieces of tape parallel on the floor. A distance of one foot should separate the two pieces of tape. This will represent an imaginary net.

o Teams must stay on their side of the tape while spreading out evenly into two rows.

o The space between the two pieces of tape is referred to as the "dead zone."

o The game starts when a member of one team serves the balloon to the other team.

o The other team tries to return the serve.

o The balloon can be hit on one side as many times as needed.

o Teams will continue to volley the balloon back and forth.

o Once the balloon hits the ground on one side, the other team gets the point and the serve.

o If the ball lands in the dead zone, the result will be a replay.

o If the same players are hitting the balloon every time, some extra rules may be added to the game (e.g., three different people have to hit the balloon before it can be passed to the other side).

o A great rule to include is that the balloon must be hit by a player in the back row and the front row before it crosses the tape/net.

o Rotate front row players, one space to the right and back row players, one place to the left after a point is scored.

o Teachers interested in making the game more challenging may implement an "elbows only" rule.

3. Locomotor relay

o Split the class into two to six teams, with no more than five students on a team.

o Clear the desks to the side or use the desks as barriers between teams.

o Have students form lines in the back of the room.

- Choose a locomotor skill, such as skipping or hopping, for students to perform as they go to a designated spot in the front of the room (possibly the chalkboard).
- One person from a team goes at a time until all members have had their turn.
- The student skips to the front of the room, skips back, and tags the next person in line.
- The goal is to be the fastest team.
- This race can be done several times while changing the locomotor movement for each race.
- If time is limited, do the race only once and change the locomotor skill at a different point in the year when you have time to do the activity again. (Refer to Chapter 5 for ideas on locomotor movements.)

4. Name pass

- Have students gather around one another to make a small tight circle with their chairs.
- Students will sit as close as possible while still maintaining a level of comfort.
- To start the game, one student will hold a ball, say their name loudly, and pass the ball to the right.
- Everyone will do this at least one or two times, with the goal of teaching everyone each other's name.
- Once all names are spoken, the game begins!
- Now, the person with the ball must say the name of the person to whom they are passing the ball.
- If the name is not said correctly, the ball should not be passed.
- If a whistle is sounded, the ball should quickly switch directions.
- The goal is to get rid of the ball as soon as you get it.
- Once students feel some success, more balls should be added to the game.
- All balls will be traveling the same direction.
- The ultimate goal of the game is *not* to be stuck with two or more balls.
- The better your students' skill level, the more balls you can enter into the game.
- If a participant is caught with more than one ball, he or she is out of the game (if the teacher chooses to play this as an elimination game).
- If you do not want to eliminate students from the game, you can invite everyone back after so many rounds.
- When the participants reenter the game, the instructor will direct them to find new seats next to different players (new names to learn).
- Having students change seats throughout the game is important so all students can learn many names.

o Alternative version: With a large group, sometimes it is more effective to make two teams: odd numbers versus even numbers. The game is played the exact same way. When someone is stuck with two balls or drops a ball, the game is stopped. If a person with an odd number dropped the ball or is stuck with two balls, the even numbered team gets the point. The opposite will be true if an even numbered person makes the mistake. Please note the emphasis is not placed on the mistake made but the skillful play of the individuals that caused the mistake.

5. Rock–paper–scissors tag
   o Split the class into two even teams.
   o A large space is needed for this activity. Options could be to clear the room, take students outside, go to the gymnasium, or find another open space in the school.
   o To play this game, all students must know how to play rock–paper–scissors. For a quick reminder, scissors (two fingers separated) cuts paper (a flat hand), paper covers rock (a fist), and rock breaks scissors.
   o Each team huddles at a designated area across the room from one another.
   o Each team must decide what their entire team will throw.
   o A few minutes will be given for each team to discuss their strategy.
   o After the discussion, each team will come to what is called the "challenge line" which is located in the center of the playing field.
   o Each team will then get in a horizontal line that is one step back from the challenge line. Both teams will be facing one another.
   o The instructor will then start the game by saying, "Rock, paper, scissors shoot!"
   o Now, team members will show the sign that they previously agreed on.
   o The team that losses the match will walk as fast and as safely as they can to a predetermined (by the teacher) safety area on their side of the room.
   o The winning team will chase the other team.
   o Any member of the team that they tag will have to come over to their side for the next round.
   o Once the new teams are formed, they will go back to their huddle to decide what sign they will use for Round 2 of the game.
   o It is interesting to see how some students react very quickly while other students will stand still because they are not sure if they should walk forward to chase or turn around to retreat for safety.

WHAT ARE NINE CLASS COHESION ACTIVITIES THAT ENCOURAGE WHOLE-GROUP UNITY?

Competing Against the Clock

1. Hula Hoop relay

   o Students will stand in a big circle while holding hands or linking forearms.

   o A Hula Hoop should be placed around any two students' arms that are linked.

   o The goal is to get the Hula Hoop around the circle without breaking the link.

   o This is a race against the clock to see how fast your class can work together to accomplish this task.

   o If you want to increase the challenge, add two Hula Hoops going in the opposite direction.

   o You can also have multiple Hula Hoops starting at different places in the link.

   o The game would end when all Hula Hoops make it around the circle one time and back to their original starting point.

2. Shoulder tap wave

   o Have students stand in a large circle while placing their left hand on the shoulder of the person on their left and their right hand on the shoulder of the person on their right. Stay linked together for the entire activity.

   o This coordination activity is like the Wave in that one person responds immediately after another, resulting in a ripple effect.

   o The first students (Student 1) will start by tapping his hand on the shoulder of the person on his left.

   o The person on the right of Student 1 (Student 2) will respond by tapping her left hand on Student 1's right shoulder.

   o The next tap comes from Student 1 as he taps his right hand on the left shoulder of Student 2.

   o The main key is the hands tap shoulders in order around the circle while creating a wave-like effect.

   o The pattern would look like this: Student 1 (left hand), Student 2 (left hand), Student 1 (right hand), Student 2 (right hand), Student 3 (left hand), Student 4 (left hand), Student 3 (right hand), Student 4 (right hand), and so on.

   o Continue the pattern until the shoulder tapping ripples around the entire circle.

   o Now, add the clock and see how fast your students can respond!

3. Pass the marble

   o Have students sit in a small, tight circle on the floor or in chairs.
   o Give one student a marble.
   o The goal is for the marble to make one complete trip around the circle in the fastest time possible.
   o If the marble is dropped, the clock is restarted.
   o The challenge of this game can be increased by adding more marbles and/or having students close their eyes to improve communication skills.

4. Over/under relay

   o Have your entire class form a straight line.
   o Give a ball to the person who is standing at the front of the line.
   o The ball will be passed through the line by going over someone's head then under someone's legs.
   o This continues until the ball gets to the last person in the line.
   o The last person runs to the front of the line and starts the process again.
   o This will continue until everyone has had a chance to be at the front of the line.
   o The goal is to race the clock to see how fast your class can accomplish this task!

5. Elbow-to-elbow

   o Have students stand in a circle.
   o Give one student a ball and ask them to pinch the ball between their elbows.
   o The goal is to pass the ball completely around the circle in the fastest time possible without dropping it (elbows only).
   o If the ball is dropped, the clock is restarted.
   o The educator can increase the challenge of this game by adding more balls to the circle.

Just-for-Fun Activities

1. Beat the pass

   o Have your students sit in a tight circle on the floor or in their chairs.
   o Leave an open space between Student 1 and Student 20 (assuming you have 20 students).
   o Student 1 will stand up, speed walk around the circle, and sit in the open spot.
   o All the other students will pass a ball around the circle while trying to keep up with the walker (Student 1).
   o When the ball gets completely around the circle, Student 2 stands up to do the speed walk.

o Everyone passes the ball around the circle again, trying to keep up with Student 2.

o The goal is for students to use teamwork as they quickly pass the ball to try to keep up with the student that is walking the lap.

o Remember to try this with various locomotor movements.

2. C-ya tag

o Clear a large area in your room (also a great game for outside).

o Before the tag game begins, place some safety spots in the game boundaries (Hula Hoops or large poster paper will work fine).

o While on a safety spot, players are safe from being tagged.

o Choose a few players to be "It," allowing them to carry a ball they can use to tag other players.

o If players are not on a safety spot, they will move around the room while trying not to be tagged by a player carrying a ball.

o If players are tagged, they take the ball, and they are now considered to be It.

o If players want to be on a safety spot, they simply step on it and say, "C-ya," to the other player on the spot.

o The other player has to get off the spot immediately.

o Note: If large safety spots are used, two players may stand on a spot at one time. In this instance, a player who wants to get on to a safety spot can simply tap the shoulder of just one of the players on a safety spot while saying, "C-ya!" (Only the player tapped on the shoulder must get off the safety spot.)

3. Don't forget my name

o Students will make a large circle with their chairs.

o All participants should sit on their chairs with the exception of one person (to simplify, the teacher may choose to be this person).

o The one person who does not have a chair stands in the middle of the circle. This person is considered "stuck."

o The person who is stuck is holding a ball.

o He or she calls out someone's name (e.g., Joe) and sets the ball in the center of the circle on the floor.

o Everyone has to find a new seat by walking quickly and safely.

o No one is allowed to take the seat to his or her immediate right or left.

o The person's name that was called (Joe) rushes into the center to pick up the ball.

o Once the ball is picked up, this person should quickly scan the room to see if someone has not yet found a seat.

o If everyone is sitting down, he or she is stuck and a new round begins.

o If people are still scattering, the person who is in the center holding the ball can call out another name of someone who has not yet found a chair.

o When students find a new seat, they stay in that seat until the round is completely over.

o The person who has the ball in the center can call only the name of someone who has not yet found a seat.

o A round is considered to be over when someone picks up the ball in the center and everyone is already seated.

o This person is considered stuck, and at this point, the next round will begin.

4. Titanic

o Begin this class cohesion activity with a discussion about the movie *Titanic* (discuss movement on the ship, the iceberg, and the lifeboats).

o The instructor will clear an area in the middle of the room and place 8 to 10 large pieces of poster board paper in a circle (Hula Hoops will also work well).

o While the teacher plays music, the students will walk or perform other locomotor movements around the pieces of paper (the deck or other areas of the ship).

o When the music stops, all students must safely get into a lifeboat (large piece of poster paper). Stopping the music simulates the crashing of the *Titanic* into the iceberg.

o The second goal of the game is that everyone must be in a lifeboat.

o Stress the idea that students should not only worry about themselves, but also they should consider the safety of all of their classmates.

o The second round of the game will now begin.

o One lifeboat will be taken away, and the teacher will turn the music back on.

o The participants will move around the ship until the music is stopped.

o Now, they will have one less lifeboat.

o The game continues by removing a lifeboat after each round.

o This gets tricky when there are not many lifeboats left, and the game becomes a problem-solving activity.

Be prepared for fun and laughter as students are engaged in the class cohesion activities explained in this chapter. As students bond, you will see strategies formed through the process of problem solving and higher-level thinking. Continue to reiterate the importance of supporting and respecting all classmates by using encouraging words and positive feedback. Bear in mind that all activities in this chapter can be altered to fit teacher/student needs. Noncompetitive games can be changed to become a means of motivation for your students. Activities that are competitive in nature can have a mere focus on fun, excitement, and movement. Class cohesion activities will provide a brain break while allowing your students to develop a unified classroom environment. This can help prepare the brain to learn at its optimal level.

Chapter 7 Recap

- Class cohesion activities are not meant for daily use in the classroom. The best time to use them is once a month for classes with a 30- to 50-minute period, once every two weeks for classes with a 90-minute period, the day after a big test, the day before or the day after a break in the school calendar, or when students are not connecting with one another.

- This book supports the idea of a balance between noncompetitive and competitive activities. However, there is more of an emphasis on activities that are noncompetitive to support the entire class working as one.

- There are two categories for class cohesion activities: (1) team unity and (2) whole-group unity.

- Class cohesion activities that build team unity occur when the teams challenge one another.

- Class cohesion activities that build whole-group unity occur when the entire class is racing against the clock or engaging in fun games together.

- There are five class cohesion activities that build team unity: (1) balloon tap, (2) balloon volleyball, (3) locomotor relay, (4) name pass, and (5) rock–paper–scissors tag.

- There are five class cohesion activities where students compete against the clock: (1) Hula Hoop relay, (2) shoulder tap wave, (3) pass the marble, (4) over/under relay, and (5) elbow-to-elbow.

- There are four class cohesion activities that are just for fun: (1) beat the pass, (2) C-ya tag, (3) don't forget my name, and (4) Titanic.

- During class cohesion activities, the importance of supporting and respecting all classmates should be reiterated by using encouraging words and positive feedback.

- Activities in this chapter can be altered to fit teacher/student needs.

8

Reviewing Content

> ⇨ How much time should be spent reviewing content through movement?
>
> ⇨ What are 20 partner or small-group movement activities that can be used to review academic content?
>
> ⇨ What are 10 whole-group activities that can be used to review academic content?

HOW MUCH TIME SHOULD I SPEND REVIEWING CONTENT THROUGH MOVEMENT?

Rehearsal, the repetitive act of processing information, is critical for transferring content from working memory to long-term storage (Sousa, 2006). Using movement to review content is a form of elaborative rehearsal, which often engages higher-order thinking skills and/or greater sensory input. Taking time to review content is an essential aspect of the teaching and learning process. Student needs differ concerning how often they require exposure to a particular concept before it is learned and stored. Many students rely on teachers to review information for recall to become more efficient. This process allows the brain to create sense and/or meaning that aids in retrieval.

Reviewing content in some form should happen on a consistent basis. A common question is how often to use movement during review. The answer depends on availability of time and type of movement activity being considered. Some activities are quickly implemented while others require more time, student involvement, and teacher-directed instruction.

These content review activities are divided between partner, small-group, and whole-group activities. Thirty different examples using movement to review various types of content for all grade levels will be presented. Some activities may need to be altered to fit a specific grade level or content area. As you read and reflect, make note of the activities that will require more time. Some movements will be more effective when large amounts of material are covered and more time needs to be devoted to its review. Others activities will align more appropriately with material that can be reviewed in a few minutes.

WHAT ARE 20 PARTNER OR SMALL-GROUP MOVEMENT ACTIVITIES THAT CAN BE USED TO REVIEW ACADEMIC CONTENT?

1. Spin to win

   o Clear a space in the center of the room.
   o Have students get into pairs.
   o Give each team four note cards labeled "A," "B," "C," and "D" (one letter per card).
   o Place several balls in the center of the room while asking all students to spread out in an equal distance away from the balls. Make sure there are fewer balls than there are teams. For example, if there are 10 teams you may want to use six balls.
   o Give all students a multiple-choice review question. Using an overhead or whiteboard to display the questions is recommended.
   o In each team, one student must discuss the possible answer with his or her partner and agree on a final decision.
   o When partners agree, the corresponding card with the correct answer is picked.
   o Students will then hook elbows and do one to three (teacher's choice) 360-degree spins.
   o After students spin around the directed number of times, one team member will run to the center of the room to grab a ball. Remember there are more teams than balls, so not every team will get a ball.
   o At the conclusion of each round, the correct answer is given.
   o Every group that got the correct answer receives one point.
   o Any group that chose the correct answer and got a ball receives an additional point (total of two points possible).
   o No points will be awarded for an incorrect answer. A decision must be made whether to give a point to teams that got a ball but had an incorrect answer.

- o Continue with a new round by placing the balls back in the center of the room and reading or showing students the next question.

2. Grab to gab

- o This game can be played on the floor or by using one desk and two chairs per team.
- o Place students in groups of two, or allow them to find a partner.
- o Partners sit directly across from each other with an object setting between them. Use a beanbag, an eraser, or something small as the object.
- o When the teacher says, "grab," or uses a distinct sound such as a whistle, both students reach for the object.
- o The student that gets the object also gets the opportunity to "gab" (answer the review question).
- o Have both students answer the question on an answer sheet.
- o The student who got the object receives two points if she answered the question correctly.
- o If the question is answered incorrectly, the object is passed over to the other player.
- o If the other player gets the question correct, he receives one point.
- o A new game is played by placing the object back in the center.

3. Fitness review

- o This game can be played on the floor or at desks.
- o Place students in groups of two to four.
- o Each group will be matched up against another group of the same size.
- o Place a pile of flip cards that contain various exercises along with the suggested repetitions (e.g., 15 crunches; refer to Chapter 6 for ideas) in the center of two teams.
- o Determine which teams will go first.
- o Read or present the chosen teams with the first review question.
- o Allow them to write their response on an answer sheet.
- o If their answer is correct, the opposing team will choose a flip card and perform the exercise on the card with the proper repetitions.
- o If the answer is not correct, they will pull a flip card and perform the exercise. While exercising, encourage students to review the correct answer in their head.
- o Now, it is the other team's turn to receive a review question.

4. Relay review

- o Clear the center of the room.
- o Split your class into four or five even teams.
- o Have each team huddle in the back of the room.

o Give the entire class the same review question.
o As a team, they must decide on an answer and send one person skipping to the board to write the answer. (Change the locomotor movement every couple of races.)
o Award one point to every team that gets the answer correct, and add an additional point for the two fastest teams with the correct answer (total of two points).
o Teams will huddle again to hear the next question.
o This time a different team member must go to the board to write the answer.
o Each relay race should have a different person racing to the board to write the team's answer until everyone has had one turn.
o The second round then begins.
o Points can be restarted, or a running score can be continued.

5. Hot potato review

o Place students into four to six even groups.
o Give each group a ball, and ask them to sit in a small, tight circle on the floor.
o Play music while students pass the ball around the circle to the person on their immediate right.
o Encourage students to pass the ball as fast as they can.
o When the music stops, all students must freeze.
o The person who has the ball has to answer a review question.
o Inform this student that he has a lifeline on his right and left; this means he can ask for help if he does not know the answer.
o This player will place his final response on an answer sheet.
o If the response is correct, he will earn a point for his team.
o The game will continue when the music is turned back on (this time the ball will be passed to the left).
o The team with the most points wins.

6. Team test

o Clear the center of the room.
o Place students in four even teams.
o Have each team sit in one of the four corners of the room.
o Give each team a written test that has questions but no answers.
o Spread note cards out in the center of the room with the answers on them face down.
o On the teachers signal, each team will send one team member racing to the center of the circle to pick up a card.
o This student is not allowed to look at the card until they get it back to her team.
o As a team, they will decide which question the answer belongs to.
o They will then send a different team member to the circle.
o This player will return the first card and grab a second one.

o As soon as he gets back to his team, they will flip the card.

o If they had this answer before, he will go back to the center, return the card, and get a new one.

o Team members caught looking at a card prior to taking it back to their team will result in a 15-second penalty for the entire team (they will not be able to go get any new card during the penalty).

o A team receiving a second offense will be given a 30-second penalty.

o The fastest team with all the correct answers wins.

7. Toss–catch review

o Place students in groups of two (three is fine if there is an odd number).

o Give each group a ball.

o Ask students to review content while tossing the ball back and forth to their partner.

8. Ordering on the move

o Place students in small, even groups. (The size and number of groups will be determined based on the content.)

o This activity is designed for information that has a specific order, such as a story line, order of operations, or a timeline of events in history.

o Give students note cards with some type of information that needs to be ordered.

o Students will line up in the proper order.

o Students will then shuffle the cards and line up again in the correct order.

o After a few practice rounds, this could easily be turned into a race.

9. Dance/lyrics creations

o Place students in groups of four or five.

o Give students academic content that you would like them to review.

o Have students create a dance and/or exercise workout along with appropriate lyrics that will help them to remember the information.

o Allow students to practice their creation for as long as deemed appropriate.

o Give the students the option to share their creations with the rest of the class.

10. Partner walk and talk

o Have students create a study guide for an upcoming quiz or test (study guide can also be provided by the teacher).

o Allow students to choose a partner.
o Set boundaries and allow students to take a walk together while discussing and reviewing the study guide.
o This activity can be done right in the classroom. However, it would also work very well outside.
o This activity can be as simple as asking students to choose a partner and walk two times around the room while sharing something that was taught in the previous lesson.

11. Multistep review

o Place students in groups of five or six.
o Have each group place their desks in a small circle.
o Give each member of the group a different, multistep problem (math would work well here).
o On the teachers signal, each group member will write the first step to solve the problem.
o After one minute, the teacher will say, "Let's move!"
o All students will stand up and begin to circle around their group's desks.
o When the teacher says, "Freeze," students will sit down in the seat they are closest to.
o Then, they will complete the second step in solving the problem.
o At any time during this activity, students who are struggling can use the person on their right or left as a lifeline.
o After one minute, "Let's move," is called out once again.
o This activity continues until all problems are completed.
o The teacher may also want to use various locomotor skills while students are moving around the desks.

12. Content area tag

o Create an open, unobstructed area to play this game.
o All students will find a partner. Students are to play this game with only their partner.
o Each pair will use a review sheet or list of questions and correct answers.
o The person who is not carrying the sheet is "It."
o This person's job is to maneuver politely through the crowd to tag his partner.
o The partner who has the question/answer sheet has a five-second head start to get away and put space between herself and her partner. In other words, "If you have the sheet, you hit the street."
o When the people who are It tag their partner, they are given a review question to answer.
o If they get the answer correct, they take the sheet, and they hit the street.

o If they get the answer incorrect, they remain It, and they must give their partner a five-second head start.

o Five minutes into the activity, ask students to get a new partner.

o Inform participants that they may use one another to dodge behind and around. However, phrases such as "excuse me" and "pardon me" are strongly encouraged. An important aspect of this game is to encourage the proper use of manners and words of kindness.

13. Vocabulary charades

o Place students in groups of four or five.

o Ask each group to sit on the floor in a small circle.

o Choose one person in each group to be the charade leader to start.

o Give each leader a pile of vocabulary words to act out and a ball for later use.

o With a two-minute time limit, the charade leaders act out the first vocabulary word they choose. They are not allowed to move past this word unless their team guesses it correctly.

o If the word is guessed correctly, the team continues to the next word in the pile.

o After two minutes, the teacher will play some music or make a distinct sound.

o This means that each team picks up a ball and begins to pass it around the circle.

o When the music stops, the person holding the ball is the new charade leader.

o Continue until a team gets through the entire pile of vocabulary words.

14. Partner ball pass review

o Allow students to get with a partner.

o Give each pair a ball and ask them to stand back-to-back.

o Have students pass the ball back and forth to each other as they continually repeat short bits of content (e.g., evaporation, condensation, precipitation, and collection—the water cycle).

o After one minute, signal students to find a new partner.

o When every student gets back-to-back with a new partner, they begin passing the ball while repeating the same information.

o Allow students to find another new partner.

o Continue this activity for only a few minutes.

15. Over and under review

o Place students in teams of six.

o Give each team a ball.

- Students will state the specific steps of the content in order as they pass the ball over their head and under their legs.
- The first person will say the first step and pass the ball over his head to the next person.
- The next person will say the second step as she passes the ball under her legs.
- This process continues until the last person gets the ball.
- This person will run to the front and say the first step again as she passes the ball over her head to the next person.
- The entire process will start over.
- This activity will continue until everyone has played every role.

16. Memory pass
    - Place students in groups of five to seven.
    - Assign one person in each group to be the team leader. Give each leader a review sheet.
    - Have groups sit in a small, tight circle.
    - Give each group a ball.
    - The person who has the ball will say a fact or information about the given content and pass the ball to the right (e.g., the periodic table, multiplication facts, and the like).
    - The job of the team leader is to listen and double-check all answers given.
    - The ball continues to be passed around the circle after correct information is given.
    - When an incorrect answer is given, the person leaves the circle for one minute to go study the review sheet (off to the side).
    - The person will reenter the game after one minute.
    - Information may not be repeated until the teacher signals the beginning of a new game.
    - At this time, the team will pick a new team leader.

17. Compare to review
    - Place students in four or five even groups.
    - Have each group sit in a designated area in the room.
    - Place signs around the room showing information to compare.
    - Give each group a note card containing information about the different topics.
    - Label the cards "Team 1," "Team 2," and so on.
    - On the teacher's signal, each group will read the first note card.
    - As a group, they will discuss which topic the information belongs to.
    - One team member is sent speed walking to tape the card on what the group feels is the correct topic. (Tape it up so that the information cannot be viewed.)

o Each team will flip one card at a time, make a decision, and send a different team member to tape it up.
o This continues until all cards are hung.
o The teacher then reviews and discusses the accuracy of the card placement.

18. Role-play review

o Divide the class into four or five even teams.
o Inform teams that they must use movement and their bodies to demonstrate three characteristics or things they would see in relation to a given topic.
o Groups will then demonstrate their creations to the entire class while explaining the different aspects of their topic.
o This is great for making comparisons.

19. Webbing on the move

o Place students in four or five even groups.
o Give each student a marker.
o Give each team a piece of poster paper.
o Allow students to tape their poster to the wall, set it on a desk, or place it on the floor.
o Have a student write and circle the topic to be reviewed in the center of each paper (the topics can be identical or interconnected).
o This activity is completely silent.
o All students must write a statement or question on the paper about the topic being reviewed.
o Students will then move to another paper of their choosing.
o When arriving at a new web, students must read it before adding their statement or question.
o The rule is read the entire web, write a question or statement, and then move to a different web.
o Continue until writing seems to diminish.
o You may also need to give verbal hints about certain information that you would like to see students recall.

20. Venn diagram review

o Place students in four even groups.
o Set up four Venn diagrams in the corners of your room by overlapping two Hula Hoops on the floor.
o Send each team to a corner with a stack of note cards that give information about the topics that are being compared.
o Students will have their own note cards.
o One student will go first by reading the information on her note card aloud and jumping into the part of the Hula Hoop that she feels is correct.

o The group will have a discussion on whether they agree with this choice.

o The second person will read his card and jump into the section of the hoop that he believes is correct.

o The group will again discuss whether they agree with this decision.

o Continue until all note cards have been discussed.

o Lead a whole-class discussion about the results.

WHAT ARE 10 WHOLE-GROUP ACTIVITIES THAT CAN BE USED TO REVIEW ACADEMIC CONTENT?

1. Volleyball review

   o This game is played with one beach ball and an obstacle that represents a net in the middle of the playing area. (Long thin tables or desks work perfectly for this game.)

   o The class is split into two even teams. One team is on one side of the obstacle while the other team is on the other side.

   o This game is set up with three rows: front, middle, and back. The beach ball is volleyed back and forth until one team allows the ball to hit the floor (you may also want to include the ceiling).

   o There is absolutely no spiking in this game! If there is an accidental spike, a replay is called. If a spike appears to be intentional, the round automatically goes to the other team.

   o The team that wins the round is given a review question. As a team, they will huddle to discuss the answer. The other team should huddle as well.

   o One student will be called on to share the team's final answer. A different player will be called on in each round to answer for the group.

   o Each question is worth two points.

   o If the team that wins the volley gets the answer incorrect, the other team can answer the question for one point.

   o One game variation is to request that the ball be touched two to three times on a side before it crosses the center: once by a player in the back row, once by a player in the middle row, and once by a player in the front row. This will increase the involvement of the participants.

   o Rotate after a point is scored.

   o Be sure that each player has the opportunity to play every position.

2. Meet and greet review

   o Students will mill around the room while saying comments such as, "Good morning," "Nice to see you," and, "How are you?"

o Encourage students to stop and shake hands or high-five one another.

o Play music during this part of the activity.

o When the music stops, have the students put their hands in the air (use a whistle if students do not notice the music being turned off).

o When students find a partner, they will high-five one another and put their hands down.

o If there is an odd number, there will be one group of three.

o Ask the students a review question.

o Give the students a few moments to discuss the answer.

o Call on one or two groups to respond and share their answer with the entire class.

o Turn the music back on and have the students begin to mill around and greet one another again.

o When the music stops, everyone will find a new partner and another review question will be given.

o This pattern will continue until all the review questions are given.

3. Musical chairs review

o Use one less desk and chair in this game than the number of students participating.

o Place review questions and a pencil on each desk.

o Have students move around the room to the beat of the music.

o Remind students to safely and carefully find a seat when the music goes off.

o When the music stops, all students will find a seat except for one.

o The students in the seats will answer the first review question.

o The student standing will take a break.

o The teacher will review the correct answer.

o When the music returns, the students will stand up and begin to walk around the room to the beat of the music.

o The student who was left standing in the first round will now sit in a chair and participate in a teacher-directed exercise (see fitness musical chairs in Chapter 6).

o When the music stops, everyone will find a seat and complete Question 2 on the review sheet.

o The one person standing will take a break.

o Review the answer with your students, and then turn the music back on.

o The student who did not find a seat in the second round will join the first eliminated student in a new fitness exercise.

o The game continues until the review questions are answered.

4. Red light–green light
   o Have students line up horizontally across the back of the room.
   o Instruct them to take one step forward when they hear a true statement while remaining still when they hear a false one.
   o Read a true/false review question to your students.
   o If the answer is true and some students step forward, tell them they are correct.
   o If a student did not step forward, explain that it was a missed opportunity.
   o If the answer is not correct and a student steps forward, they must go back to the starting line.
   o If they did not move forward on a false statement, inform them of their correct decision.
   o Continue until review questions are depleted or any number of students make it to the designated finish line.

5. Bingo review
   o Give students a blank bingo card with approximately 20 squares (a word bank may be added to the top of the card).
   o Be sure to number the squares 1 through 20.
   o Give each student a review question turned upside down so it cannot be seen.
   o Be sure to have some duplicates of each question.
   o Spread out the pile of duplicates at a designated area in the room.
   o There is absolutely no talking in this game.
   o On command, students flip over their question.
   o They will match the number of the question to the number of the square on the bingo card.
   o Students will attempt to answer the question while writing their response in the appropriate box.
   o They will then speed walk to the designated area to replace their question with a new one.
   o Students are not allowed to look at the new question until they get back to their seat.
   o Students who look at the cards prematurely will receive 15 seconds in the penalty box (a specified area in the room).
   o A second offense will result in a 30-second penalty.
   o If they get a question they already completed, they must hustle back to the designated spot to replace it.
   o Any student who has a bingo card full of correct answers at the end of the allotted time wins.

6. Cardio review
   o This activity can be used for reviewing multiple-choice questions.
   o Choose a cardiovascular exercise for answers A, B, C, and D (refer to Chapter 5 for ideas).

o For example, A might be jumping jacks, B box jumps, C squat jumps, and D mountain climbers.

o Present the class with a review question.

o Allow them to answer by performing the cardiovascular exercise that represents their choice.

o It will be easy to see which students know the correct answer.

o Review the correct answer and move on to the next question.

7. Match maker

o Place words and their definitions on note cards.

o Give every student a note card.

o Allow them to stand up and circulate around the room to find their match.

o Continue until everyone has a match.

o Mix up the cards and play again.

o Do this numerous times.

8. Freeze dance and fitness freeze review

o This is a variation of freeze dance (Chapter 5) or fitness freeze (Chapter 6).

o Have students dance or exercise to music.

o When the music goes off, have students sit in their seat and answer one or two review questions.

o When the music is turned back on, have students stand to dance or exercise.

o Repeat pattern until review questions are completed.

9. Down the line

o Split the class into two even teams.

o Have one team stand directly across from the other team while facing one another.

o Give a review question and allow the students facing one another to discuss the answer.

o After a few minutes, have one or two groups share their answers.

o Have each group take one step to their right so they are facing a new partner.

o Give the second review question.

o Share answers and have each group take one step to their right again.

o Continue until all questions are reviewed.

10. Comparison review

o Place signs in different areas of the room that list different topics or subtopics that your students are learning about.

o Read a statement that describes one or many of the topics.

o Students will stand and go to the topic that they believe is being described.

- o If the statement reflects more than one topic, students will go to the center of the room and point to the topics they believe are being described.
- o Review answers and lead appropriate discussions after each statement.
- o Continue until all questions are reviewed.

Chapter 8 Recap

- Rehearsal is critical for transferring content from working memory to long-term storage (Sousa, 2006). Using movement to review content is a form of elaborative rehearsal, which often engages higher-order thinking skills and/or greater sensory input.

- Reviewing content in some form should happen on a consistent basis.

- The content review activities in this chapter are divided in two sections: (1) partner or small-group activities and (2) whole-group activities.

- This chapter contains 30 review activities that incorporate movement.

- Some activities may need to be altered to fit a specific grade level or content area.

- The 20 partner or small-group activities are as follows: (1) spin to win, (2) grab to gab, (3) fitness review, (4) relay review, (5) hot potato review, (6) team test, (7) toss-catch review, (8) ordering on the move, (9) dance/lyrics creations, (10) partner walk and talk, (11) multistep review, (12) content area tag, (13) vocabulary charades, (14) partner ball pass review, (15) over and under review, (16) memory pass, (17) compare to review, (18) role-play review, (19) webbing on the move, and (20) Venn diagram review.

- The 10 whole-group activities are as follows: (1) volleyball review, (2) meet and greet review, (3) musical chairs review, (4) red light–green light, (5) bingo review, (6) cardio review, (7) match maker, (8) freeze dance and fitness freeze review, (9) down the line, and (10) comparison review.

9

Teaching Content

⇨ Should I read and consider all the movement activities in this chapter even if they are not in my content area?

⇨ What are eight movement activities that can be used to teach and learn English concepts?

⇨ What are eight movement activities that can be used to teach and learn math concepts?

⇨ What are eight movement activities that can be used to teach and learn science concepts?

⇨ What are eight movement activities that can be used to teach and learn social studies concepts?

SHOULD I READ AND CONSIDER ALL THE MOVEMENT ACTIVITIES IN THIS CHAPTER EVEN IF THEY ARE NOT IN MY CONTENT AREA?

Yes! You never know what information will trigger a creative thought. Education is cross curricular with a strong spiral profile. Reading through an activity not related to your field might inspire you to contemplate something you teach. Activities may need to be altered to fit your needs, but a number of ideas can originate from one activity. Many ideas and/or movement activities are often transferable. An activity used in science could match with information taught in English or social studies. Sometimes, connections are made in the brain when we least expect it.

The goal of this chapter is to inspire your creative process about how your content can be taught through movement. As explained in Chapter 1, creating movement activities can be challenging, as it requires creative thought. The key is the willingness to teach in a nontraditional manner. It can seem difficult at first, but know that it is expected. With patience, more ideas will come over time. When planning your lessons, remember to ask yourself, "Can I teach this academic concept through movement?" Sometimes the answer will be no, but you might be surprised how well movement lends itself to the teaching and learning process.

As an expert in your subject area, and as you read about your content area in this chapter, allow your perspective to broaden as you consider everything you teach. With some thought and planning, you can build on these ideas and make them fit your needs. Continue to think about your students. By putting yourself in their shoes, you can imagine how it would feel when participating in the various activities. Once you see the increase in learning efficiency, you will be more motivated to expand the opportunities for teaching content through movement.

You might also consider activities that are not related to your content area by asking yourself, "Can this activity be used to teach information in my subject area?" Creative ideas will come more easily as you continue to design your activities and alter ones that are presented here. Teaching and learning through movement is an inventive resource that is well worth the time it takes to develop and perfect. Finally, many of these movement activities are meant to accompany what you are already doing in the classroom. Continue to explain, model, practice, and/or demonstrate your academic content. However, make time for movement, as your students' brains and bodies desire and need it!

WHAT ARE EIGHT MOVEMENT ACTIVITIES THAT CAN BE USED TO TEACH AND LEARN ENGLISH CONCEPTS?

Elementary English

1. Editing on the move—punctuation and mechanics
   o Allow students to work alone or with a partner.
   o Give each student or group a list of sentences that need to be edited.
   o Have each person or group walk while editing one sentence at a time.
   o To demonstrate the editing, students should do the following:
      a. Have students raise their hands in the air to demonstrate a capital letter.

    b. Have students pause for commas and slightly bend their knees.

    c. Have students add a punctuation mark at the end of each sentence. The period will be demonstrated by going into the tuck position (bend down and hug your knees). The exclamation mark will be shown by jumping up and down on both feet at the same time. To demonstrate the question mark the students will stand on one leg and make a hook-like action with the opposite arm. Also, apostrophes will be added by lifting the right arm and making a hook-like action.

o After all sentences are completed, the participants will compare their edited sentences while discussing any differences they have.

2. Puzzle pattern—reading comprehension and order of events

o Place 20 spots or laminated pieces of paper on the floor.

o Make five rows across and four rows down. (This can be smaller or larger depending on your grade level and material you are using.)

o Place laminated note cards on the spots that describe the order of events that happened in a story.

o Inform your students that they will jump (or step) to each spot based on the order of how things happened in the story.

o Have students form a half circle (a line) around the pattern on the floor so that everyone can see what is happening.

o There is no talking at any time.

o Every spot will only be stepped on one time.

o Students can only step to the right, left, front, back, or diagonal from the spot that they are currently on. (They cannot jump two spots.)

o The first person steps on a spot that he feels shows the first thing that happened in the story. The teacher will either say, "That is correct; you may take another step," or "I am sorry, but that is not correct."

o When the person is incorrect, he goes to the end of the line and a new person steps on the first spot.

o Students will continue to move through the pattern until they take an incorrect step.

o Everyone should pay close attention to see where the mistakes are being made so they are not repeated.

o Eventually, everyone in the class will go through the sequence of events.

o This activity also works well in smaller groups with two to four puzzle patterns around the room.

3. Building a plot diagram—sequencing

o Prepare for this activity by taping large plot diagram shapes to the classroom floor and creating sets of index cards with short stories broken up into the five plot parts. However, if the class is split into teams of seven students, for example, seven index cards must be created per story. Therefore, there may be more than one exposition, rising action, falling action, and/or resolution card.

- o Model this activity with the class.
- o Have the students help you decide where to place each index card (part of a story) on the diagram.
- o Read the story aloud and have the students determine if any changes in placement are needed.
- o Students will work in teams of five or more.
- o Have them start by labeling the five parts of the plot diagram with a marker.
- o Next, each student will be given an index card with a portion of the story's plot written on it.
- o They must work together to determine which part of the story each teammate has.
- o When they agree, they should place their index cards along the appropriate sections of the diagram and read the story aloud.
- o They should determine if any changes are needed.
- o The teacher will verify the accuracy of the plot diagram.

4. The descriptive writing hop—descriptive writing and sentence structure

- o Separate your class into six teams (Team 1 will play against Team 2, Team 3 against Team 4, and Team 5 against Team 6).
- o Make flip cards containing various topics (vocabulary words will work well).
- o Place 10 paper plates per team in a straight line (30 paper plates).
- o Have Team 1 line up on one side of the first paper plate, with Team 2 on the other side.
- o Have the first member of Team 1 pick a flip card.
- o She must design a descriptive sentence about that topic.
- o She hops alongside the paper plate for each word of the sentence.
- o All players listen carefully for accuracy.
- o When the student is finished, the points are tallied.
- o Now, the first member of Team 2 takes his turn (flip a card and hop out a descriptive sentence).
- o Then it goes back to the second member of Team 1.
- o Allow students to keep a running score as they hop to create their descriptive sentences.

Secondary English

5. Prepping for persuasive writing—the writing process and communication

- o Have students find a partner.

o Allow each pair to mill around the room to find an object that can be held in their hand.

o Now, give each pair five minutes to build a persuasive sales pitch for their object.

o Have partners decide who will play the role of a consumer and who will be a salesperson.

o Give each salesperson a sales slip that a customer will sign if he or she would buy the object.

o Students will stand up and circulate around the room.

o Consumers will walk around while waiting to be approached by a salesperson.

o Students playing the role of the salesperson will take their object and try to sell it to as many consumers as they can by using verbal communication and body language.

o Consumers interested in buying the object must sign the sales slip.

o After five minutes, have partners switch roles.

6. Character analysis—literary analysis

o Tape short stories all around your classroom.

o Give each student character analysis sheets that include some or all of the following: protagonist, antagonist, minor character, static character, dynamic character, explicit judgment, and implied judgment.

o Each student will walk around the room reading the stories and completing a character analysis sheet for each story.

o To add more movement and creativity to this activity, assign students a character to play from one of the stories.

o Allow them to walk around the room while pretending to be that character without telling others who they are.

o They can discuss parts of the story without giving too much detail, use appropriate language from the correct time period, and use body language to show who they are.

o After an appropriate amount of time, you can have students stand, one at a time, and play "Who am I?"

o Allow other students to guess the character while labeling his role in the story.

7. Kinesthetic character analysis—in-depth character analysis

o Ask students to find a partner.

o Each partner will face one another and have the job of describing a literary character through kinesthetic analysis as follows.

o Pointing to their heads, students describe the character's most important thoughts.

o Pointing to their eyes, students describe the lens through which the character sees the rest of the world.

o Pointing to their mouths students describe the most critical elements of the character's personality.
o Pointing to their shoulders, students describe the burdens the character carries.
o Placing their hands over their hearts, students describe the character's love interests and any emotional traits.
o Folding their arms, students describe any physical labors the character endures.
o Putting their hands over their stomach, students describe any situations that make the character very nervous.
o Touching their legs, students describe the important travels of the character.
o Bending down and touching their toes, students describe what philosophies and beliefs ground the character.

8. Modern-day Shakespeare—recreation of literary works
   o Students will recreate Shakespeare's work by designing scripts that translate each scene of an act into a meaningful, relevant, modern-day play.
   o For example, read each segment of *Macbeth*. A common framework to study the play looks like this.

   Act I, Scenes I–IV

   Act I, Scenes V–VII

   Act II, Scenes I–II

   Act II, Scenes III–IV

   Act III, Scenes I–III

   Act III, Scenes IV–VI

   Act IV, Scenes I–III

   Act V, Scenes I–XI

   o Now place students in manageable groups. Newly designed scripts based on modern interpretation of thematic material (the witches in Macbeth have been known to be cab drivers, gossip girls, or television personalities) are given as homework, generally a scene per night, and performed the next day in class.
   o The major life themes in *Macbeth,* such as greed, pride, jealousy, and revenge, are just as relevant today as they were in Shakespeare's time.
   o A helpful tip is to create a wiki (an online collaboration tool) so students can communicate about the development of their scripts in the evening while at home.
   o Movement is only a part of this assignment but an important part that helps bring these creations to life by taking student ideas from the page to the stage.

WHAT ARE EIGHT MOVEMENT ACTIVITIES THAT CAN BE USED TO TEACH AND LEARN MATH CONCEPTS?

Elementary Math

1. Clusters—addition, subtraction, multiplication, word problems, and square roots

   o Have students walk in a clockwise circle around the leader (teacher).
   o Announce a math problem using addition, subtraction, multiplication, division, or a word problem.
   o The job of the students is to get in a cluster that tells the answer to a given problem. For example, if the instructor gave the example of 1 + 1, all students would get into clusters of two as quickly as possible.
   o The teacher would recognize a cluster because the participants are standing close together with their arms linked to one another.
   o If students are unable to get in a cluster of the correct number, they are eliminated from the game.
   o Instructors can continue to play this game as an elimination game, or they can allow the players back into the game after a few rounds.
   o When students are not playing in a round, have them perform fitness activities or use flip cards to practice their math skills.

2. High–low fitness roll—number sense, place value, and probability

   o Place participants in four even teams. Use a piece of poster paper to show the following:

      1. __ __ __, __ __ __, __ __ __
      2. __ __ __, __ __ __, __ __ __
      3. __ __ __, __ __ __, __ __ __
      4. __ __ __, __ __ __, __ __ __

   o Each team will take turns rolling the dice to try to get the highest or lowest number on the board.
   o There will be two winners in each round (highest and lowest).
   o The first number may not start with a zero.
   o If a 10 is rolled, it is equal to 0 while 11 and 12 are equal to 1.
   o Team 1 will roll the dice.
   o As a team, they will have one minute to make a decision and send one person to place the number on the board. He must say the correct place value as he puts the number on the board.
   o Once the number is placed on the board, the team will choose a fitness activity from a list in the room and perform the activity for the same number of times as the number they rolled (a different exercise must be chosen each time around).

o Team 2 then takes their turn followed by Teams 3 and 4.

o During the second round, it is important that a different team member rolls the dice and discusses the placement of it on the board.

o Please note that every participant is responsible to roll the dice and place the number on the board after discussing it with her teammates.

o After a team wins, its members can stay out of the game until another team places second.

o When two winners are decided, the game is over, and it is time to begin another round.

o The teacher can stop the game at any point to present the class or team with a question regarding probability.

3. Finding surface area—area and similar math problems

   o This activity requires four packets of square-feet paper. (Square-unit paper may also be used depending on the teacher's objective.)

   o The goal of this activity is for students to discover the formula for surface area.

   o Explain a square foot to your students.

   o Divide students into four groups.

   o Distribute one packet to each group.

   o Demonstrate how to show a 5 by 5 (five across and five down) on the board.

   o Have students move to create their five by five using the packets while spreading out their squares on the floor.

   o Have students use the squares to fill in the area so it is entirely covered.

   o Have students count the squares (each group should have 25 squares).

   o Write 5, 5, and 25 on the board.

   o Repeat the previous steps for a 4 by 6 and 3 by 7.

   o At this point, you should have the following written on the board:

   5, 5, 25

   4, 6, 24

   3, 7, 21

   o Review the four possible operations: (1) addition, (2) multiplication, (3) division, and (4) subtraction.

   o Have each group decide what operation could be used to solve these three problems mathematically.

   o Discuss this with the whole group.

   o Next write 6 by 4 on the board and have students predict the area (24).

   o Groups will then check their answer using the squares.

   o Repeat this for 3 by 7.

   o Ask students to come up with a possible formula for surface area (multiply length by width).

4. Learning fractions—fractions

o Prior to this lesson, make red and blue headbands for students to wear (half the class wears red, half wears blue).
o Use fraction cards with one fraction on each. The numerator will be written in red and the denominator in blue.
o Divide your class into two teams. Each team has half of the members wearing red headbands and half of the members wearing blue headbands.
o Review numerator and denominator.
o Hold up one card.
o Each group will create a human fraction that represents the fraction on the card.
o Do three cards as practice to allow students a chance to ask any questions about the rules before you make it a game.
o Hold up a card.
o The group that creates the human fraction first receives two points, and the other group will receive one point for the correct answer.
o Discuss each problem with the whole group.
o Be sure to use cards for this lesson that will work with the number of students in each class.
o Allow students to switch the color of their headbands halfway through the activity.
o Use this activity as a warm-up to more difficult questions with fractions, such as having students demonstrate ⅓, ½, or ¾ of their group.

Secondary Math

5. Solving an equation—any multistep math problem

o Put students into teams of six or seven.
o Make a set of laminated numbers zero through nine, an x for the variable and +, −, =, / signs for each group.
o Have one team come to the front of the room to demonstrate how to solve an equation with a variable while using movement and their bodies.
o Give the demonstration group signs with which to work.
o By using their bodies and holding the signs in front of them, students will get in a straight line and show the equation.
o Show the class how to solve this equation while the students use their numbers and signs to show each step of the process.
o Each group member will have to move around to show each step.
o After this demonstration is completed, it is time for the groups to try it with their team.
o Give each team a set of the laminated cards and four or five equations to solve.

o It would be very easy to continue this activity with problems of a higher difficulty level.

6. Additive inverse race—locating, ordering, and understanding a relationship between positive and negative numbers

o Make 10 black and 10 red construction paper cards for each team (about the size of an index card).

o Make three to five sets of number cards for each team on white paper. Number cards should include negative and positive numbers.

o Separate the class into two to three even teams (8 to 10 students per team).

o Give a set of number cards to each team containing one card for each team member.

o Explain that each team will participate in the activity at the same time.

o Have a team leader pass out a white number card to each team member. Teams cannot look at their number or anyone else's until the timer is started.

o Without talking, students need to form a line in order from the least to the greatest.

o While forming their line, students with negative numbers on their card must also hold a red card along with their number card. Students with positive numbers will hold a black card along with their number card.

o While standing in their number line, any students who represent an additive inverse should squat down on the floor.

o The team that completes the task the fastest earns two points. One point will be given to the other teams that have the correct answer.

o Number cards will be collected and Round 2 will begin with new number cards for each team. (Number cards can also be recycled to other teams later in the game.)

o The teacher can determine how long this game will be played based on the number of white positive and negative card sets that are created.

7. Finding the circumference and diameter of a circle—circumference and diameter

o Create enough space for all students to form a circle.

o Have one student walk heel to toe around the entire circle making sure to count his steps and finish at the same spot where he started.

o At the original starting point have that same student turn toward the circle (the students should open the circle) and walk a straight line from one side of the circle to the other, heel to toe and counting all of his steps.

o That student has just marked both the circumference and diameter of a circle. The relationship is pi. The general equation is the circumference of a circle is a bit more than three times the diameter of the same circle (pi = 3.141).

o Doing this kinesthetically could produce an inexact result but will be close enough to teach the concept.

o If walking the entire circle produced 27 steps and walking the diameter produced 8.5 steps, the result would be 3.176.

8. Similar triangles—triangles and other geometric shapes

o Have five students stand side by side, each about five feet apart.

o They should stand with large cards labeled this way:

   B   D   A   E   C

o Ask the students to the immediate left and right of the center (Students D and E) to take three steps forward.

o Ask Students B and C to take six steps forward. The group will have formed a triangle. (Student A in the center has not moved.)

o Next, ask a student of the correct height to lie between Students D and E, who have walked forward three steps.

o Then ask a taller student to lie between the students who walked forward six steps (Students B and C).

o You have created two similar triangles (see Figure 9.1).

Figure 9.1 Similar Triangles

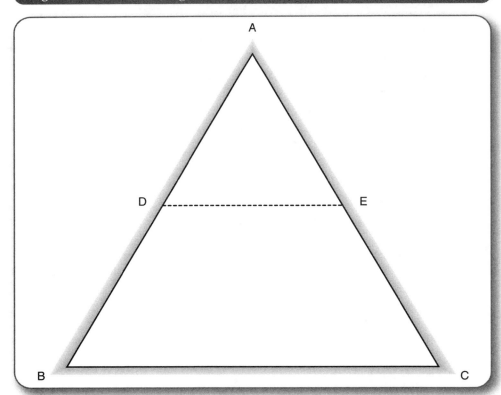

o In summary, when Students D and E are the points of intersection of a line parallel to the bottom of the triangle (connecting Students B and C), with sides connecting Students A and B and Students A and C, respectively, then triangle A-B-C is similar to triangle A-D-E.

WHAT ARE EIGHT MOVEMENT ACTIVITIES THAT CAN BE USED TO TEACH AND LEARN SCIENCE CONCEPTS?

Elementary Science

1. Animal cells—parts of an animal cell and their functions

   o Place students in two groups (Number 1 and Number 2).
   o The Number 1s will be on the inside circle moving clockwise.
   o They will be responsible for acting out what the cell part looks like.
   o The Number 2s will be on the outside circle moving counterclockwise.
   o They will be acting out the cell part's job. Students will move around in their circle.
   o The teacher may use music during this part of the game.
   o When the music stops, call out the name of a cell part.
   o Students will have to find their partner and act out the cell part and its job.
   o The last pair of students to find their partner and act out the cell part are eliminated from the game for one round (have them do fitness activities or view a study guide).
   o Here are the motions for the game.

Cell Part	Appearance Action	Job Action
Nucleus	Located in the center of the cell, has a circular shape (students grab their knees and make the shape of a ball)	Is the "brain of a cell" and controls all functions (students point to their brain)
Mitochondria	Mighty mitochondria (students make a muscleman pose)	Creates energy (students jump and down)
Vacuole	Shaped like a circle (students hold their hands out in front of them like they're holding a beach ball)	Stores things within the cell (students step into their partner's basket)

(Continued)

(Continued)

Cell Part	Appearance Action	Job Action
Cell membrane	Surrounds the cell, like a gate **(students link arms with a partner)**	Regulates what goes in and out of the cell **(students link arms with a partner)**
Cytoplasm	Fluid-filled space—the "soup" **(students make a stirring motion like they're stirring soup)**	Controls cell metabolism **(students make a stirring motion like they're stirring soup)**

2. Becoming the water cycle—ordering of events
   - o Divide students into two groups.
   - o Each group will need to demonstrate or become the water cycle.
   - o To represent evaporation, groups will get on their knees and link hands to show a body of water. They will slowly stand to show how that water changes to steam and vapor.
   - o The groups must decide how many students are needed to play this role.
   - o Someone also needs to represent the sun's job in this step.
   - o Condensation can be demonstrated by students acting like clouds.
   - o Students can show precipitation by dancing their fingers like rain.
   - o Teams will need to use all members to show the different steps of the cycle.
   - o Students will rotate until everyone has a chance to be each stage.

3. Producers, consumers, and decomposers tag—the food chain
   - o Divide your class into three groups for a tag game: (1) plants, (2) prey, and (3) predators.
   - o Clear a large area in your room or take your students outside.
   - o Make signs that label their roles to tape on your students' chests.
   - o Most of your students will play the role of the producers (plants).
   - o In this game, they will be stationary. When they are tagged by prey, they are out of the game.
   - o There are two consumers: (1) predator and (2) prey.
   - o The prey is a smaller group than the producers.
   - o They will walk (or jog) in the designated area to try to tag the producers while avoiding the predators. When they are tagged by a predator, they go off to the side and decompose (break down and shrink).
   - o The predators are the smallest group.
   - o They will move around while trying to tag the prey.
   - o When all of the players who are prey are dead and decomposing, they can start to tag one another.

- When predators are tagged, they will also go over to the area on the side to decompose.
- Play a few games so students can play each role.

4. Seismic waves—density and traveling waves

- Divide the class in half and have them stand in a line across from one another on either side of the room.
- On one side, the students should stand shoulder to shoulder (close equals dense material), and on the other side, the students stand an arm (or two arm's) length apart (farther apart equals less dense material).
- This provides a visual for what it means to be dense.
- Next, have all students put their hands out in front of them, palms up.
- On the count of one, starting at the same end of each line, have the students tap one another's hand going down the line, simulating a seismic wave traveling through this particular layer of the Earth's core.
- The students who are standing closer together will have their wave travel to the end faster, showing that the denser (more solid) the material, the faster the waves travel through this layer.
- Students can then switch roles to experience the other densities and how fast, or slow, the waves travel.

Secondary Science

5. Neural network relay race—neurons or order of events

- Divide your class in half.
- There will be two neural networks racing against each other.
- Each neural network will be made of two neurons.
- Make note cards describing the job of each person or part of the neural network.
- The number of students in your class will determine how many people play a particular role. Player's roles are as follows:
  a. Dendrite of the first neuron: One to three people spread their arms out to show that a dendrite can have many branches (like a tree)—their job during the relay is to observe.
  b. Nucleus of the first neuron: One person will be prepared to catch a ball that is thrown to him by the leader of the game (the teacher or another classmate)—the ball represents a new piece of information that is exciting the nucleus of the neuron. This person says, "Bzzz," as he catches the ball and passes it to the next person.

     c. Axon of the first neuron: One person or group (as many people as needed) will stand in a straight line, shoulder-to-shoulder—explain that their clothing is like the myelin sheath (insulates the neuron from other neurons, increases speed of impulse, and prevents the electrical current from leaving the axon). As the ball comes to them, they pass it down the line as quickly as possible—they say, "Pass it down," repeatedly to show that the electrical impulse is carrying the new information down the axon.

     d. Synaptic gap of the first neuron: One or two people pass the ball (the electrical impulse) chemically (neurotransmitter) from one neuron to the next—they say, "From one neuron to the next."

     e. Dendrites of the second neuron: One to three people receive the ball (the electrochemical impulse) from the synaptic gap—they then pass the ball to the axon. They say, "Give it to the axon."

     f. Nucleus of the second neuron: One person is just an observer (this person contains genes and cell history). You can have them cheer for the dendrites to pass the information (ball) down the line more quickly.

     g. Axon of the second neuron: One person or groups (as many people as needed) will stand in a straight line, shoulder-to-shoulder—explain their clothing is like the myelin sheath. As the ball comes to them, they pass it down the line as quickly as possible—they say, "Pass it down," repeatedly to show the electrical impulse is carrying the new information down the axon. The last person of the axon throws the ball to the leader and the process starts again.

- This is a timed relay race (two to three minutes).
- The teacher stands between the two neural networks.
- At the start of the race, the leader throws a ball to the first nucleus, of each team, at the same time.
- When the ball is thrown to the nucleus, it represents the idea that when we attempt to learn something a neuron is stimulated or excited. During the three minutes, each team will send the ball (the information) through the neural network as quickly and as many times as possible.
- At the conclusion of the three minutes, everyone will freeze (using a whistle may be a good idea here).
- See which group moved the information through the neural network the fastest. Explain the importance of repetition when learning a new piece of information.

6. Calculating for speed—speed or mathematical comparisons

- Separate the class into four equal relay teams.
- Explain the formula for speed that we will be used in this activity: average velocity = total distance traveled(m)/total time(s).

o Give each student a worksheet for calculating speed.

o Explain that each group will have the opportunity to experience four different relay races as well as calculate their speed for each one.

o At the conclusion of the activity, groups will share their average speed for each race.

o The instructor can lead the class through a discussion on comparing the scores to see which groups had the fastest speed per station.

o The stations are as follows:

a. Ball hop: Students will squeeze the ball between their legs and hop down to the end line and back. The distance used will be four meters. After the race, team members must go directly to the instructor to receive their time.

b. Gallop: Students will gallop down to the end line and back. The distance used will be seven meters. After the race, team members must go directly to the instructor to receive their time.

c. Karaoke/grapevine: Students will stand sideways and use the pattern cross in front, cross behind, cross in front, cross behind down to the end line, and back. The distance will be six meters. After the race, team members must go directly to the instructor to receive their time.

d. Partner front-to-front walking: Two participants will face one another and lock forearms. Therefore, one player will be moving forward while the other player will be walking backward. Together, they must go down to the end line and back. Each participant must go two times. The distance used will be five meters. After the race, team members must go directly to the instructor to receive their time.

o Run one relay race at a time. (Playing upbeat music during the races also makes things fun!)

o After all relay races are completed, allow students to calculate their average speed for each race.

o Then have students compare their answers with their teammates'.

o Compare scores to find the team with the fastest average speed per race.

o Finally, have students calculate their average speed of all the races.

7. Meet, greet, and write a chemical formula—chemical formulas

o Make cards with ion symbols printed on them.

o Pass out the cards to students.

o Explain that while the music is on students are to walk at a medium speed around the room greeting one another with an appropriate remark.

o When the music stops, students find the oppositely charged ion closest to them.

o Together, the two students (a positive and a negative ion) must decide what proportion they will combine in, decide on the name and chemical formula for the compound they would form, and be ready to tell the teacher or their neighboring pair.

8. Exploration of density and comparison of phases of matter—density and phases of matter

o Make three equal boxes (approximately 2 feet by 4 feet) on the floor using the tape.

o Ask 4 or 5 students to stand in the first box and 8 to 10 students to stand in the second box.

o Question students about the following:

a. Who can compare the volume of the two boxes in which students are standing? (They are the same.)

b. Which is more crowded? (The one with more students is more crowded.)

c. Imagine each student represents one particle (such as an atom or molecule) of matter. For example, let's say the first box contains four atoms of aluminum and the second box contains eight atoms of lead. The density of the first box is less than the density of the second box.

o Use the term "particle" and the visual representation to write a definition of density (density is how tightly packed particles are for a given volume).

o Now ask six to eight students (particles) to stand in each box.

o Identify Box 1 as solid, Box 2 as liquid, and Box 3 as gas.

o Instruct particles to follow directions given.

o Ask volunteers to read the following:

a. When matter is in a solid state, the particles are close together, have a fixed shape and fixed volume, and because the temperature is comparatively low, they barely move—just vibrate in place.

b. As heat is added and a solid melts to form a liquid, the thermal energy is converted into kinetic energy and the particles begin to slip and slide over one another—they spread out filling the bottom of the container first. The volume doesn't change, but the shape is determined by the container.

c. As more heat is added and a liquid evaporates to form a gas, more thermal energy is converted into kinetic energy, and the particles can now move as far apart from one another as possible. They use all the space of the container and frequently bump into the sides of the container and one another. There is no definite shape or volume to a gas.

o Repeat with new particles.

WHAT ARE EIGHT MOVEMENT ACTIVITIES THAT CAN BE USED TO TEACH AND LEARN SOCIAL STUDIES CONCEPTS?

Elementary Social Studies

1. Cardinal directions—directions and map familiarity

   ○ Have participants pretend the classroom is a map.
   ○ Their bodies are compasses.
   ○ Read the story.
   ○ When the word "north" is spoken, the participants will begin to walk to the front of the room.
   ○ When the word "south" is spoken, participants will walk to the back of the room.
   ○ When the word "east" is spoken, participants will move to the right of the room.
   ○ When the word "west" is spoken, participants will move to the left of the room.

STORY

(Read slowly, accentuating the cardinal directions giving the students time to move.)

I woke up one Saturday morning and decided that I wanted to take a trip, but I didn't know where to go. Should I go *south* toward warm weather? Should I go *north* to see Niagara Falls? Should I go *west* to Ohio to ride one of my favorite roller coasters at Cedar Point? Or should I go *east* to see my friends in New Jersey? There are so many wonderful things to see and do that I just couldn't make a decision.

Finally, I decided to bounce a penny onto my map and follow its path. The penny landed on Niagara Falls, so I began to head *north*. On my way there, I decided to take a "small" detour and headed *east* to Bar Harbor, Maine. After a day of whale watching, I headed *west* back toward Niagara Falls. It was very wet! What should I do next? I wondered. Then I realized that I had never seen a flamingo! So I headed *south* to Florida. I was so hot there that, after a little while, I knew that I needed to go somewhere cooler.

I decided to go to Mammoth Cave in Kentucky. I figured that a cave would be cool. But oh my! I had a problem. Kentucky wasn't in just one direction but two from Florida! What was I to do? Then it hit me! I would go in both directions at the same time! Boy! Am I smart or what? I traveled *northwest*

(Continued)

(Continued)

and found the cave. The cave was fun for awhile, but then I decided to visit my friend, Cowboy Sam. So I headed *southwest* to Dallas, Texas. Sam wasn't home so I decided to travel *northeast* to Washington, D.C., to see the White House. That got me thinking about the presidents so I headed *northwest* to Mount Rushmore in South Dakota. It was amazing!

I heard about a famous bridge in San Francisco, California, so I headed *southwest* again to see the Golden Gate Bridge. Guess what. It's red!

I decided to head *north* to Seattle, Washington, and went in the Space Needle. Wow, was I high. I started to feel hungry when I heard my mom call me to come for dinner. We were having hot dogs, so I didn't want to be late. I quickly headed *southeast* and was home and eating hot dogs in a flash!

2. Communities—urban versus rural or other comparisons
   o Split the class into two teams with one-third on one team and two-thirds in the other.
   o Have the small group stand in a large area of the room.
   o Have the large group stand in a small area of the room.
   o Discuss some differences between rural and urban communities.
   o Ask students to consider differences that have not been discussed.
   o Now, divide the class into four or five even teams.
   o Inform teams that they must use movement and their bodies to demonstrate three characteristics or things they would see in a rural and urban community.
   o Groups will need six demonstrations, three for each community.
   o Groups will then perform their demonstrations for the other groups while explaining the different aspects of each community.

3. The conquering of the Aztecs—war
   o Split the class into two teams.
   o The Aztecs will consist of two-thirds of the class while the Spanish conquistadors will consist of the other one-third.
   o Choose a leader for each team and set the boundaries for the game.
   o The designated area for the game is known as Tenochtitlan.
   o The leader of the Aztecs will be called Montezuma.
   o The leader of the conquistadors will be Hernando Cortez.
   o After choosing team leaders, explain the rules of the war (tag game).
   o The first rule is that the Aztecs are only allowed to walk at a regular pace.
   o The conquistadors will be allowed to speed walk or gallop (depending on space) to represent the horses that they used to aid in their victory over the Aztecs.

o Second, the conquistadors will be allowed to use shields (books) to block the Aztecs when they attempt to tag them.

o Aztecs will not be able to use shields.

o Third, the conquistadors will be given balls that they can use to tag the Aztecs.

o These balls will represent bullets.

o Red balls that are used will represent smallpox.

o The fourth rule, which really makes the game, is both teams will move around the designated area trying to tag one another.

o If a conquistador tags a player on the Aztec's team with a ball (bullet or smallpox), the Aztec is considered dead and must leave the game immediately.

o If an Aztec tags a conquistador, the latter simply loses that body part and can no longer use it in the game.

o If conquistadors are tagged in the back or stomach, they lose their ability to move; however, they are still alive.

o The second time they are tagged, they are dead and they leave the game.

o During this war, it was believed that many of the Aztecs switched sides and joined the conquistadors after being persuaded by an Aztec woman named Doña Marina.

o It is even suggested that Montezuma may have been killed by one of his own men.

o Therefore, throughout the game, the teacher will play the role of Doña Marina by handing balls to some of the Aztecs and turning them into conquistadors.

o The game is finished when Montezuma is dead and most players have a ball and have become conquistadors.

o The region where the game originated (Tenochtitlan) was renamed New Spain after the war and is known as Mexico today.

4. Major wars with United States involvement—understanding sequencing of events and timelines

o Give four students each a large index card with the year 1700, 1800, 1900, or 2000 written on it (one card per student).

o Ask the students to stand and get into the proper time sequence from 1700 to 2000 (left to right). Now, ask them to spread apart so there is enough space between centuries for other students to stand.

o Hand out the following cards to 10 students (one card per student) representing United States involvement in major wars.

American Revolution (1775–1783)

War of 1812 (1812–1815)

Civil War (1861–1865)

Spanish-American War (1898)

World War I (1914–1918)

World War II (1939–1945)

Korean War (1950–1953)

Vietnam War (1960–1975)

Persian Gulf War (1990–1991)

Iraq War (2003–present)

o Based on the dates given, ask students to line themselves up correctly in the proper centuries.
o Students should be in the correct order within the correct century.
o Have all students read their cards (including century) in the correct order from the beginning of the timeline to the end.
o Do as many times as necessary to involve all students.

Secondary Social Studies

5. Dynastic cycle circle—the Chinese dynastic cycle or events that have a repetitive pattern

   o Explain the different steps of the dynastic cycle.
   o Have the students use movement to experience or demonstrate each step.
   o Split students into teams of six.
   o Give a ball and index cards that explain the different steps of the dynastic cycle to each group.
   o Each student in a group will take a card.
   o Then have students form a circle with each student getting in the correct order based on the information on her card.
   o Have students pass the ball around the circle. The person with the ball will act out his part of the cycle.
   o The cycle will continue until the dynasty has both come to power and been overthrown. Students will then create a new dynasty or simply rotate cards to play another role in the cycle.

6. Chivalry game—how squires became knights, student behavior, and social interaction

   o Each boy in this class is now a squire or knight in training and will be training to become knights under _____'s (teacher's name) kingdom.
   o Boys are to follow the rules of the chivalry game and earn enough points to become one of King _____'s brave and courageous knights.
   o Boys (squires) are to act courteous in all encounters with the girls (maidens) under the kingdom (school), for the entire Middle Ages unit.
   o This may include the following: carrying such things as books, book bags, or lunches, opening doors, picking up dropped materials, pulling out chairs, helping with homework, and the like.

- o Girls (maidens) are to keep tallies of each squire's acts of courtesy toward them.
- o These tallies are to be put into the box in the classroom at any time the young maidens wish.
- o Any acts of discourtesy are to be reported to King _____.
- o At the end of the unit, each squire with 30 or more acts of courtesy will be knighted and given a piece of land under the Kingdom.
- o The knight with the most acts of courtesy in each class will earn the special title of lord of the manor (class period).

7. Electoral college—state comparisons and multiple civic lessons

- o Point out that the number of electoral votes a state receives is also based on the number of congressional representatives it has in the House of Representatives.
- o This leaves Oregon with 7 total electoral college votes and Pennsylvania with 21.
- o Based on numbers, any two states can be represented.
- o The physical size of a state and its relationship to the number of votes it receives can also be examined.
- o For instance, a very large state like Montana has only 3 electoral college votes because of its small population and small representation in congress (give three students a very large part of the room), and a much smaller state like New York has 31 electoral college votes because of its much larger population density (put all remaining students in a much smaller area of the room).

8. The law of supply and demand—supply and demand

- o Ask one student to stand and be the producer of a good or service.
- o Give the student a ball that represents this good.
- o She is given 10 more balls to represent her continued success at creating this product.
- o Next, have a group of five students stand in the center of the room. They will represent consumers and will be interested in this new good.
- o The producer will set a price of $1.00 for her good.
- o Have two consumers purchase this good.
- o The producer still has eight products left to sell, but the two consumers who purchased the product loved it and told the other three consumers who also told two friends each.
- o Now, nine consumers want the remaining eight products, which will bring us to our first law of supply and demand: As demand for a product rises and supply falls, the price of a product will also rise.
- o The producer decides to produce much more of her product—give the producer 20 balls—and charge $1.50 for this product.
- o Have 20 students each purchase this product at $1.50.

o With the product being very successful, the producer decides to raise her price once again to $2.00.

o Consumers decide that they are not willing to pay this price, and the producer has excess inventory, which brings us to the supply side of this law: As demand falls and inventory rises, prices drop.

o The $1.50 price is known as a market-clearing price: a price that was determined by market fundamentals and deemed fair to all by natural market forces.

o This lesson could extend to include the producer, middleman, retailer, and consumer.

Chapter 9 Recap

- Read all movement activities in this chapter because you never know what information will trigger a creative thought in your brain.

- Education is cross curricular with a strong spiral profile.

- The goal of this chapter is to inspire your creative process about how your content can be taught through movement.

- Allow your perspective to broaden as you consider everything you teach. With some thought and planning, you can build on these ideas and make them fit your needs.

- Teaching and learning through movement is well worth the time it takes to develop and perfect.

- These activities can accompany or replace what you are already doing in the classroom.

- Eight movement activities that can be used to teach and learn English concepts are (1) editing on the move, (2) puzzle pattern, (3) building a plot line, (4) descriptive writing hop, (5) prepping for persuasive writing, (6) character analysis, (7) kinesthetic character analysis, and (8) modern-day Shakespeare.

- Eight movement activities that can be used to teach and learn math concepts are (1) clusters, (2) high–low fitness roll, (3) finding area, (4) learning fractions, (5) solving an equation, (6) additive inverse race, (7) finding the circumference and diameter of a circle, and (8) similar triangles.

- Eight movement activities that can be used to teach and learn science concepts are (1) animal cells; (2) becoming the water cycle; (3) producers, consumers, and decomposers tag; (4) seismic waves; (5) neural network relay race; (6) calculating speed, (7) meet, greet, and write a chemical formula; and (8) exploration of density and comparisons of phases of matter.

- Eight movement activities that can be used to teach and learn social studies concepts are (1) cardinal directions, (2) communities, (3) the conquering of the Aztecs, (4) major wars with the United States, (5) dynastic cycle circle, (6) chivalry game, (7) electoral college, and (8) the law of supply and demand.

10

What Matters Most

➪ What are three developmental stages of life that are consistently measured throughout the infancy and elderly years?

➪ What are the three learning domains of education, and how are they connected to the developmental stages?

➪ How might this connection apply to my teaching in regard to the six purposes of movement?

WHAT ARE THREE DEVELOPMENTAL STAGES THAT ARE CONSISTENTLY MEASURED THROUGHOUT THE LIFESPAN?

Recall the last time you watched a child grow and develop. Whether it was one of your own children, a niece, a nephew, or even a grandchild, you probably paid very close attention to different stages of development. It is human nature for us to compare children to one another as we evaluate these different stages. There are three stages that we monitor the closest: (1) cognitive, (2) social, and (3) psychomotor (physical). We ponder concerns such as the following: "Shouldn't they already know their ABCs?" "Why aren't they capable of playing nicely with other children?" "Why isn't my child walking yet?" We use these comparisons to decide if children are acting, growing, moving, and thinking appropriately for their age. We may get excited when children are ahead of a typical standard or feel concerned if they appear to be falling behind. The bottom line is these three areas matter most in regard to the development of the children in our life.

These three developmental stages are so important to us that we spend a great deal of time trying to improve them as soon as a child is born. We read to children; we sound out words and teach them what items, objects, and colors are called. This is an initial attempt to build cognitive skills. We talk in cute voices, make funny faces, and smile just to make a baby laugh. We can't wait to see how their personality is going to take form. This is the initial development of social skills. We bounce children, help them to stand, and balance them as they begin to walk. These are the first efforts in improving physical growth. If we detect a sign that children are struggling in a particular area, we respond by devoting more time and effort to their needs. The timely growth in these three areas is significant to the child and to the people who care for and love the child.

Now let's consider what matters most when someone becomes elderly. Aging or spending time with someone who is growing old can be very difficult. The three most important considerations are the same as with a child: (1) cognitive, (2) social, and (3) psychomotor (physical) well-being. We take note to their cognitive ability. Can they remember their family member's names? Are they capable of taking their medication without constant reminders? We pay attention to see if elderly people are getting out, socializing, and maintain connections with their friends. We monitor their physical capabilities. Can they walk without help? Can they get in and out of the shower without assistance? These three areas are major factors in determining the quality of their life. Elderly people who are maintaining cognitive, social, and physical well-being have a much better chance of enjoying the later years of their life.

WHAT ARE THE THREE LEARNING DOMAINS OF EDUCATION, AND HOW ARE THEY CONNECTED TO THE DEVELOPMENTAL STAGES?

When it comes to education, there are three separate learning domains: (1) affective, (2) cognitive, and (3) psychomotor. Following are descriptions of these domains:

1. Cognitive domain: This domain involves knowledge and the development of intellectual skills.

2. Affective domain: This domain includes the manner in which we deal with things emotionally.

3. Psychomotor domain: This domain includes physical movement, coordination, and the use of motor skills.

These learning domains directly coincide with the three developmental stages that are of the utmost importance. The cognitive domain overlaps with the cognitive stage in that the focus is on gaining and retaining knowledge. Being able to develop and maintain intellectual skills is of great significance. The affective domain is tied to the social stage in that acting appropriately while dealing with and expressing emotions is a desired life skill. Improving listening and communication skills will play a vital role in building relationships. The psychomotor domain is identical to the psychomotor stage because movement, balance, and self-care help create independence and personal health, which is essential to life.

HOW MIGHT THIS CONNECTION APPLY TO MY TEACHING IN REGARD TO THE SIX PURPOSES OF MOVEMENT?

Take note to the previously mentioned statement regarding the developmental stages in the infancy and elderly years. What about the school years? Are cognitive, social, and psychomotor skills developed daily throughout the school day? The answer to this question will depend on the teacher. Do you have a cognitive, affective, and psychomotor objective in every lesson you teach? All teachers have cognitive standards that they aim to reach on a daily basis, but does this mean that the social and psychomotor domains are forgotten?

You may be saying, "Isn't the psychomotor domain the physical education teacher's responsibility?" Of course it is, but this task requires a unified approach, and considering the small amount of physical education some students receive, it merits consideration from all teachers. The physical education teacher is also responsible for the affective and cognitive domains, as they build social skills and cover content. As discussed in Chapter 1, many children are overweight and out of shape. This concern will require support from the entire education system if this problem is going to diminish. In addition, by incorporating the six purposes of movement into every lesson, cognitive, social, and physical skills can be built.

Imagine writing your daily lesson plans and incorporating three objectives consistently. The academic standard will be your first consideration. This is appropriate. However, don't stop there. Think about what other objectives you would like to have students meet in your classroom. What social skill would you like to encourage? In what physical activity would you like students to engage? An example of a written objective for the affective domain is, "Students will work cooperatively in the beat the pass class cohesion activity." An example of a written objective for the psychomotor domain is, "Students will actively participate in beat the pass while skipping, hopping, and sliding."

This philosophy truly supports the idea of educating the child as a whole. As you write your lesson plans, make an effort to have at least one objective from each of the three learning domains. You will find that as you incorporate the six purposes of movement you will provide an environment where cognitive, social, and physical learning takes place. Teachers are already doing an outstanding job with developing children's cognitive abilities; now is the time to focus on physical and social growth as well. After all, these three areas matter most in our lives!

Chapter 10 Recap

- Three developmental stages matter most in the infancy and elderly years: (1) cognitive, (2) social, and (3) psychomotor (physical).

- There are three learning domains in education: (1) cognitive, (2) affective, and (3) psychomotor (physical).

- The three learning domains directly coincide with the three developmental stages.

- Teachers should consider writing three objectives in every lesson plan, one for each learning domain.

- This philosophy supports the idea of educating the child as a whole.

- Teachers are already doing an outstanding job with developing children's cognitive abilities; now is the time to focus on physical and social growth as well. After all, these three areas matter most in our lives!

Resources

Belknap, M. (1997). *Mind body magic: Creative activities for any audience*. Duluth, MN: Whole Person.

Blakemore, C. L. (2003). Movement is essential to learning. *Journal of Physical Education Recreation and Dance, 74*(9), 22–28.

Brady, L., King, B., Martinez, E., Milbert, F., Sweeney, D., & Valero, D. (2008). *Action based learning lab: Strategy for successful student achievement data explanation*. Prince William County Public Schools, AAHPERD National Convention, April 11, 2008.

Bunker, D., & Thorpe, R. (1982). A model for the teaching of games in secondary schools. *Bulletin of Physical Education, 18*(1), 5–8.

Burden, P. (2006). *Classroom management: Creating a successful K–12 learning community*. Hoboken, NJ: John Wiley & Sons.

Burnette, E. (2009). *The impact of physical activities on reading vocabulary skills among K–2 special education students* (Unpublished master's thesis). Gratz College, Melrose Park, PA.

Burr, S. (2009). *The effect of kinesthetic teaching techniques on student learning* (Unpublished master's thesis). Gratz College, Melrose Park, PA.

Caine, R., & Geoffrey C. (1994). *Making connections: Teaching and the brain*. Menlo Park, CA: Addison-Wesley.

Campbell, L., Campbell, B., & Dickinson, D. (2004). *Teaching and learning through multiple intelligences*. New York: Pearson.

Gardner, H. (1983). *Frames of mind*. New York: Basic Books.

Gastler, S. (2009). *Kinesthetic strategies and the development of phonological awareness* (Unpublished master's thesis). Gratz College, Melrose Park, PA.

Glover, D. R., & Midura, D. (1992). *Team building through physical challenges*. Champaign, IA: Human Kinetics.

Goleman, D. (1995). *Emotional intelligence: Why it can matter more than IQ*. New York: Bantam.

Graham, G., Holt-Hale, S., & Parker, M. (1993). *Children moving: A reflective approach to teaching physical education*. Palo Alto, CA: Mayfield.

Greenleaf, R. K. (2003). Motion and emotion. *Principal Leadership, 3*(9), 14–19.

Hula Hoop®, a registered trademark of Wham-O, Inc.

Kaye, P. (1984). *Games for reading*. New York: Pantheon Books.

Kirchner, G. (1992). *Physical education for elementary school children*. Dubuque, IA: Wm. C. Brown.

Lutz, J. (2009). *Using kinesthetic components to enhance student involvement in the social studies classroom* (Unpublished master's thesis). Gratz College, Melrose Park, PA.

Malone, D. (2009). *The impact of the phonics dance on kindergarten students* (Unpublished master's thesis). Gratz College, Melrose Park, PA.

Matwijiw, S. (2009). *The impact of nutrition and physical activity on academic performance* (Unpublished master's thesis). Gratz College, Melrose Park, PA.

McNutt, L. (2009). *The empact of kinesthetic-based activities on student understanding of the eight parts of speech in the seventh grade English classroom* (Unpublished master's thesis). Gratz College, Melrose Park, PA.

Morris, D., & Stiehl, J. (1999). *Changing kids games.* Champaign, IL: Human Kinetics.

Ober, K. (2009). *The effects of brain gym on the reading fluency of third, fourth, and fifth grade learning support student* (Unpublished master's thesis). Gratz College, Melrose Park, PA.

Pangrazi, R. P., & Dauer, V. P. (1995). *Dynamic physical education for elementary schools.* Boston: Allyn & Bacon.

Rohnke, K. (1984). *Silver bullets: A guide to initiative problems, adventure games, Stunts and trust activities.* Dubuque, IA: Kendall.

Rohnke, K., & Butler, S. (1995). *Quicksilver.* Dubuque, IA: Kendall.

Rubinstein, G. (1999). *Reluctant disciplinarian: Advice on classroom management from a softy who became (eventually) a successful teacher.* Fort Collins, CO: Cottonwood Press.

Saxton, M. (2009). *The importance of using music and movement in the kindergarten classroom* (Unpublished master's thesis). Gratz College, Melrose Park, PA.

Smolinsky, B. (2009). *The effects of kinesthetics on the acquisition and retention of the French language* (Unpublished master's thesis). Gratz College, Melrose Park, PA.

Tomlinson, C. (1999). *The differentiated classroom: Responding to the needs of all learners.* Alexandria, VA: Association for Supervision and Curriculum Development.

Traubel, D. (2009). *The impact of bodily-kinesthetic strategies on math skills in a first grade classroom* (Unpublished master's thesis). Gratz College, Melrose Park, PA.

Weikel, A. (2009). *The effects of kinesthetic teambuilding activities on students with emotional disturbances* (Unpublished master's thesis). Gratz College, Melrose Park, PA.

Williams, N. F. (1992). The physical education hall of shame. *Journal of Physical Education, Recreation and Dance, 63*(6), 57–60.

Wolfe, P. (2001). *Brain matters, translating research into classroom practice.* Alexandria, VA: Association for Supervision and Curriculum Development.

Wood, N. (2009). *The impact of movement on the student's ability to retain information* (Unpublished master's thesis). Gratz College, Melrose Park, PA.

Wootan, F. C., & Mulligan, C. H. (2007). *Not in my classroom: A teacher's guide to effective classroom management.* Avon, MA: Adams Media.

References

Adams, J. (2009). *The impact of kinesthetic activities on eighth grade benchmark scores* (Unpublished master's thesis). Gratz College, Melrose Park, PA.

Blaydes Madigan, J. (1999). *Thinking on your feet.* Murphy, Texas: Action Based Learning.

Blaydes Madigan, J., & Hess, C. (2004). *Action based learning lab manual.* Murphy, Texas: Action Based Learning.

Bruer, J. T. (1991). The brain and child development: Time for some critical thinking. *Public Health Reports, 113*(5), 98–387.

Burr, S. (2009). The effect of kinesthetic teaching techniques on student learning (Unpublished master's thesis). Gratz College, Melrose Park, PA.

Dennison, P. E., & Dennison, G. (1988). *Brain gym, teachers edition.* Ventura, CA: Edu-Kinesthetics.

Gibbs, S. (2009*). Using bodily-kinesthetic activities to foster student success in a high school Spanish classroom* (Unpublished master's thesis). Gratz College, Melrose Park, PA.

Glasser, W. (1998). *Choice theory: A new psychology for personal freedom.* New York: HarperCollins.

Gold, P., & Sternberg, E. (2002, April). The mind-body interaction in disease [Special edition]. *Scientific American,* 8.

Hannaford, C. (1995). *Smart moves: Why learning is not all in the head.* Marshall, NC: Great Ocean.

Harding, T. (2009). *Using gross motor activities to increase the attention span of early intervention students with developmental delays* (Unpublished master's thesis). Gratz College, Melrose Park, PA.

Healy, J. (1990). *Endangered minds: Why our children don't think, and what to do about it.* New York: Touchstone Rockefeller Center.

Hubbard, J. (2009). *Kinesthetic mathematics instruction for secondary students with traumatic brain injury* (Unpublished master's thesis). Gratz College, Melrose Park, PA.

Jensen, E. (1998). *Teaching with the brain in mind.* Alexandria, VA: Association for Supervision and Curriculum Development.

Jensen, E. (2000). *Learning with the body in mind.* San Diego, CA: The Brain Store.

Kinoshita, H. (1997). Run for your brain's life. *Brain Work, 7*(1), 8.

Kissler, A. (1994). *On course: Games for everyone.* Auburn, CA: On Course.

Medina, J. (2008). *Brain rules.* Seattle: Pear Press.

Mitchell, M. (2009). *Physical activity may strengthen children's ability to pay attention.* University of Illinois at Urbana-Champaign: News Bureau.

Oberparleiter, L. (2004). *Brain-based teaching and learning.* Department of Education, Gratz College. Graduate Course Trainers Manual. Randolph, NJ: Center for Lifelong Learning.

Pica, R. (2006). *A running start: How play, physical activity, and free time create a successful child.* New York: Marlowe and Company.

Promislow, S. (1999). *Making the brain-body connection: A playful guide to releasing mental, physical, and emotional blocks to success.* Vancouver, BC, Canada: Kinetic.

Putnam, S. C. (2003, February). Attention deficit: Medical or environmental disorder? *Principal Leadership, 3*(6), 59–61.

Queen, A. J., & Queen, P. S. (2004). *The frazzled teacher's wellness plan: A five-step program for reclaiming time, managing stress, and creating a healthy lifestyle.* Thousand Oaks, CA: Corwin.

Ratey, J. (2008). *SPARK: The revolutionary new science of exercise and the brain.* New York: Little, Brown and Company.

Schmitt, B. D. (1999). *Your child's health: The parents' one-stop reference guide to: symptoms, emergencies, common illnesses, behavior problems and healthy development.* New York: Bantam Books.

Shade, R. A. (1996). *License to laugh: Humor in the classroom.* Westport, CT: Teachers Idea Press.

Sousa, D. (2006). *How the brain learns.* Thousand Oaks, CA: Corwin.

Sprenger, M. (1999). *Learning and memory: The brain in action.* Alexandria, VA: Association for Supervision and Curriculum Development.

Sternberg, E., & Gold, P. (2002). The mind-body interaction in disease: The hidden mind [Special edition]. *Scientific American, 12*(1), 82–129.

Sullo, B. (2007). *Activating the desire to learn.* Alexandria, VA: Association for Supervision and Curriculum Development.

Sylwester R. (1995). *A celebration of neurons: An educator's guide to the human brain.* Alexandria, VA: Association for Supervision and Curriculum Development.

Texas Education Agency. (2009). *Overview.* Retrieved from http://www.cooper institute.org/ourkidshealth/documents/Data%20Overview—3-9-09.pdf.

Winterfeld, A. (2007). PE makes a comeback. *State Legislatures Magazine, 33*(10), 36–37.

Wood, N. (2009). *The impact of movement on the student's ability to retain information* (Unpublished master's thesis). Gratz College, Melrose Park, PA.

Index

CORWIN

A SAGE Company

The Corwin logo—a raven striding across an open book—represents the union of courage and learning. Corwin is committed to improving education for all learners by publishing books and other professional development resources for those serving the field of PreK–12 education. By providing practical, hands-on materials, Corwin continues to carry out the promise of its motto: **"Helping Educators Do Their Work Better."**

RTC's mission is to provide high quality graduate courses that empower teachers with knowledge, skills and strategies to enhance classroom instruction.